ENGINEMEN
ELITE

ENGINEMEN ELITE

ELITE

NORMAN McKILLOP

("Toram Beg")

A Goodall paperback
from
Crécy Publishing Limited

First Published 1958
© Norman McKillop

This Edition published 2023
Copyright © Crécy Publishing Ltd 2023

ISBN 9781800352858

Printed in Malta by Melita Press

Front cover:
BR (ScR) 60535 'Hornet's Beauty' Edinburgh Waverley 19 July 1958. *OTA*

A Goodall paperback
published by

Crécy Publishing Limited
1a Ringway Trading Estate, Shadowmoss Road, Manchester M22 5LH
www.crecy.co.uk

Contents

Foreword 6

Chapter One   The God in the Bowler Hat..7

Chapter Two   Cleaning to Kill 17

Chapter Three   Lodging Turn—Old Style 28

Chapter Four   A Spare Life but a Gay One 39

Chapter Five   An Era Ends 50

Chapter Six   C'est la Guerre 61

Chapter Seven   Where every Prospect Pleases 66

Chapter Eight   A New Conception 78

Chapter Nine   Big Bill Stevenson 90

Chapter Ten   Life with "Swannie" 98

Chapter Eleven   Speed Merchants All 109

Chapter Twelve   The Badge of the Bowler Hat 120

Chapter Thirteen Mainly North Eastern...130

Chapter Fourteen "Spearmint" and I 140

Chapter Fifteen   Performance Plus 151

Chapter Sixteen   War and all that 164

Chapter Seventeen The "Why" is Important 171

Chapter Eighteen Goodbye to "Spearmint".......................................180

Conclusion..187

Foreword

This story is mainly concerned with a bunch of "top link" express engine drivers, who from a rather nondescript beginning, through good humour, hard knocks, and occasionally travail, became fashioned to the respectable eminence, described by one writer as the *"elite* of enginemen" on the East Coast route between Edinburgh and London.

When it was suggested that an autobiography might prove readable, I felt that the time wasn't just ripe for such an effort on my part, but as far as it goes this book *is* biographical to the extent that it covers nearly forty years personal experience of engines and men, at a depot which became the main Scottish stable for the Gresley Pacific engines.

This book, however, is not solely concerned with these superb locomotives and the driving of high-speed engines. There is a great deal more than this in an engineman's career, and in recording this I am hopeful that I have achieved two things, *(a)* to express the thoughts of an engine driver, and *(b)* the reason for these thoughts.

I leave it with the reader to judge whether I have succeeded.

N. McK.
Edinburgh, 1957

I

The God in the Bowler Hat

The first time I ever rode on a locomotive at the head of a train, it cost me the price of one ounce of tobacco—three pence! That possibly, better than anything, paints the picture of our railways in 1910. It was an easy existence where rules and regulations were concerned; but our standard of living was represented by one golden sovereign each fortnight as wages for 120 hours of work, and a careless acceptance of the fact that if you were engine-daft, as I was, you were bound to the locomotive for every one of your waking moments—literally every moment.

That three pence worth of tobacco was illustrative of this dedication. I had worked a full shift as greaser in Haymarket goods yard (where I'd been banished by the Locomotive Foreman at the engine sheds for reasons which I'll state later) and the tobacco was a grateful token to the fireman on the St. Boswells goods for allowing me to do all his work for a further ten hours on what was the biggest class of goods engine on the North British system of those days.

It was an eighteen inch cylinder type, with a rounded cab, No. 182: and it and Bobby Baillie were almost one and indivisible. "Bobby Baillie" may sound a gay, rapturous sort of label for any individual to carry around, but whoever corrupted "Robert" into the juvenile "Bobby" had no sense of the fitness of things. Bobby always gave me the impression that he was dressed in striped trousers, frock coat and top hat, leading one of the more decorous processions of deacons—and he acted accordingly. By no stretch of imagination could you ever conceive him as being anything but dignified—and No. 182 was similarly inclined.

On the "St. Boswells" it was considered little short of sacrilegious by "Bobby" even to think about opening the "big" valve. No matter what the load, as the train wound its way through the hills and valleys (and some of the hills had gradients of 1 in 70) the throttle was never opened further than the full extent of the "wee" valve, with innumerable graduations between that and "shut." Fortunately for Bobby and 182 there were scattered all over their route many hill pilot engines which, while merely supposed to assist trains, got most of the work to do on the "up" bits, while on the descending gradients and the level, 182 meandered sedately along. It was the only engine I've ever ridden to which I felt inclined to apply the detested term "puffing."

To fire to Bobby Baillie on the "St. Boswells" was considered the easiest thing in Haymarket. He drove this train daily for more years than I can remember, so this first stolen run on the footplate couldn't have been very exciting in reality. But to my daft mind it was the height of pulsating adventure (rather dampened, I admit, every time I looked at Bobby's phlegmatic and absolutely immobile countenance).

It's a long forty-six years ago, but every wheel turn of that trip is still vivid in my mind. There was the slow, almost imperceptible start away; the crawl across four sets of main line rails with the signalman watching our inching progress with resigned patience, and me pitching coal feverishly into the small square firebox as if it was an Atlantic engine with nearly eight feet of grate length. It is true to say that the only noise created by that engine from first to last of the trip was that of my clattering amateur attempts at firing, until I was stopped by the fireman. During the whole trip, as far as I can remember, not one word was spoken by Bobby either to the fireman or to myself and I got it into my head that somehow or other we had become invisible to him. That, I may say, was not an unusual characteristic of many of the Scots drivers of those days. They were by no means garrulous.

So I thoroughly enjoyed myself. I fired the engine, I kicked on the water regulator at floor-level, and turned the flat circular steam key on the storm-board to work the injector. I was allowed to twist on the tender hand-brake as we hit a delirious 25mph on the speediest bit, and convinced myself that I was surviving a pretty hectic experience with marvellous *sang-froid* and indomitable courage. All this was on top of a full working shift, and then I went home that Sunday morning and lay in bed for hours going over every momentous and wonderful minute of the trip.

That was how engine-daft I was. That also gives an indication of the mental approach of some of the old time drivers. They were a law unto themselves. Bobby Baillie and all he represented put his engine first and foremost. It was *his* engine, not the property of the N.B.R. He and his ilk would see the timetable far enough, rather than do what they considered harmful to their engine. If the full wee valve meant crawling at 10mph rather than running at 20, then the train crawled, and neither guard, signalman, or "gaffers" could make them alter the pace.

Maybe that is why they stayed on the "goods", for in those days promotion was not automatic as it is nowadays. The "gaffer" had a big say in that; which brings me to the reason why I joined the locomotive department to become a driver, yet found myself greasing wagons in a goods yard, the slave of "Shorty" the wagon examiner.

I was suffering punishment for daring to speak back to "Big Jim" Lawrie, the Haymarket shed "gaffer." The yarn is perhaps interesting for three facts: (a) I think I can claim to be the only one who ever told "Big Jim" what I thought of him and remained un-sacked; *(b)* it points the full autocratic power wielded by the shed foreman of those days; and *(c)* that curiously, on the former North British, the wagon examiners were in the locomotive department, not the carriage and wagon department as they are today.

I have told elsewhere the yarn about my first contact with James Lawrie, the Shed Foreman at Haymarket in 1910. He was a rather terrifying figure to my skinny immaturity when he first took me on, as I thought, to clean engines, then fire them and in the dim future to drive them. "Big Jim," six feet three and as like "Buffalo Bill" as two peas, had other ideas. In the account I have written of that period I declared that he tested me out in engine fireboxes for six months before he was convinced I was tough enough for the footplate.

Actually I jumped a lot of detail in that account.

When I started at 6pm on my first day, I found that I was condemned to service in the store. Here I issued oil and cotton waste, tallow and bathbrick, flax and corks, and a multitude of weird things, in the uses of which I hadn't the remotest idea or interest. Nor was I interested in the telephone to which I was supposed to attend, in between my other duties. I hadn't left a job with a whole shilling a week more than I was going to get at Haymarket to act as counter-hand at any store. No, I wanted close and intimate contact with railway engines: and, skinny or not, railway engines I was determined to have.

The result was inevitable. Somewhere in my background were "Hielan't rebels" and this must have driven me on, much to "Big Jim's" astonishment I guess; for I learned later that even the toughest thought twice before "crossing the gaffer." In my callow ignorance I walked where strong men (if not angels) feared to tread. I walked into "Big Jim's" office and stated my desires.

He never even turned his head to look at me. "Away an eat mair parritch!" he boomed out; and somehow his voice lifted me out of the "presence." That was the start of a long series of pestering, ineffective attempts on my part to get out of that unhallowed store, until "Big Jim" got tired of it. "Come into this office once more", he warned me, "and your name will be Norman Walker not McKillop." After that what could I do? The sack would have been the end of the world to me. Then I hit on a bright idea. "Big Jim" hadn't forbidden me to *write* my demands, so I pushed a note under his office door every day until one day the door was yanked open and a hand like a mechanical shovel scooped me up and set me down inside the office with a force which made my teeth rattle. Electric sparks were coming from "Big Jim's" eyes, moustaches and goatee beard, and making all my spinal discs fall out of place.

"Here's a line, you little 'so and so' nuisance," he said. "Into the office and get your money—you're sacked! And heaven help you if I see your face again. You'll never make a driver—its real men we need for that job."

Well, here it was—I'd shot my bolt; but I'd tried. Then something inside me blazed, and I can still see the look in "Big Jim's" face. "Maybe you're big," I yelled at him, "maybe you're strong, but there's one thing you aren't—you're not fair. You've never even tried me to see if I was fit. If you were a man at all you would put me on the hardest job a cleaner does, then sack me if I can't do it." Having eased my soul, I made for the door at speed.

I was in the act of bringing the door shut with as vicious a bang as I could manage when I thought I heard a voice. "Here," it called. It was so quiet I doubted my ears. It wasn't "Big Jim's" boom.

I opened the door and he was standing with his hand outstretched. "Give me that line," he demanded. If he'd wanted to frighten me he couldn't have succeeded more. There was sheer menace in his tone. (Years later I apologised to him, for no one on earth had the right to tell Jim Lawrie that he "wasn't *a* man at all"; that, however, is by the way.) I handed him the chit. "Now get back to your work. I'll attend to you later," was all he said; and I scuttled like mad.

At the end of that week there was a curt note handed to me by the clerk. "Start on Monday as greaser in Haymarket yard" was all it said—but I knew that "Big Jim" had started to try me out.

"Shorty" the wagon examiner obviously had his instructions, although never once did he admit it. That he was summoned to the "presence" I do know, and when he returned from that interview with Jim Lawrie he was obviously briefed.

I knew by the signs. When we carried a wagon drawbar "Shorty" took the lighter end, I carried the end with the hook and coupling attached, and learned the hard way how to lift heavy weights with the minimum of effort. In point of fact, once I tumbled to the fact that the hard way was to be my lot, I hit on a great truth, delivered out of the mouth of an old Scottish locomotive inspector who liked to orate. "Let every 'deefeeculty' be your opportunity," he declaimed, and I revelled in my martyrdom.

I expended a prodigious amount of energy showing off to "Shorty." In secret I practised with wagon axle-boxes until I could grab them off the ground with the gayest of abandon, carry them up and down the yard, scorning such aids as barrows, until I'm sure "Shorty" thought I was as daft as I really was.

My heart was grieving for the engine-shed, but I had little opportunity of even poking my nose inside, although it was little more than two hundred yards from the goods yard. "Shorty" saw to it that I was kept busy.

I spent months bent double under wagons, renewing springs, brake rods, and draw-gear. I learned how to fit axle-boxes, wagon door hinges, end plates, buffer beams, and even renew a pair of wheels—but *above all I greased wagons;* and how I hated that soapy mess and the double compartmented tin box and flat heavy "knife" which were the tools for the job. I used to imagine what I'd like to do with "Shorty" and the grease to which he seemed devoted. I would bury him to the neck in one of his barrels, I would then push his head slowly and relentlessly down, and nail the lid on. Then I'd roll the unholy stuff with "Shorty" embedded firmly in it down the bank, and watch it burning in the town incinerator nearby.

Little did quiet decent Jim Short know the rebel who in silence ate his sandwiches in the "bothy" which served us as mess-room, store-house, workshop and office. (It was merely the sawn-off half of a freight van minus the wheels—not even a window lightened its gloom). When we dined here, we did so in an aroma of carriage oil and the everlasting grease, and I often wonder if my good digestion is perhaps due to the soda I must have swallowed along with my "piece" during this period of my railway career, for strong soda seemed to be the chief constituent of the wagon lubricant supplied to the N.B. examiners.

Mixed with sand, it was used to wash our hands and must have had some curative effect, for my hands were never free of cuts and abrasions from my abandoned use of them in repairing wagons, and all the treatment they eve received was a Spartan scrubbing with "yellow butt" (as Shorty called the grease) and sand. It was a pretty painful operation, but it cured all right, and so far as I can recollect nobody suffered from the dermatitis so common nowadays among people handling oil.

I could not get near the engine shed, so I had to make do with the next best thing, the Haymarket shunting pilot, and even here "Shorty" cramped my style. Thinking he would not mind, I worked like a Trojan to finish the jobs in hand, then sneak a ride on the pilot. "Shorty," however, had other ideas; the more I "horsed" through the work the more he produced to keep me from wearying, and it was only by cutting an already meagre mealtime that I could indulge my consuming passion on N.B. "pug" No. 39.

Number 39 was a saddle-back "tanky" and was destined later to be the first regular engine on which I fired (although by the time that happened I had fired for odd days on other pilots as a cleaner-fireman). When I was attached to "Shorty" one of the regular drivers was Andrew Manzie, who was later to be my first mate.

"Andra" had a way with youngsters, and welcomed my stolen moments. He had come off the main line passengers for health reasons, but this was hard to believe, for to shunt on these pilot engines year in and year out was no light undertaking. There was no cab whatsoever. Rain, wind, sleet or snow, the Haymarket pilot never stopped; and exposure to a Scottish winter for ten hours a day needed some stamina—I know that from bitter experience, "bitter" being the operative word in this connection.

"Andra" must have been sheer iron—indeed, *was* sheer iron, as I found out later, but what mattered to me was his good nature and his welcome when I first climbed the steps of his engine. He sensed my ignorance and told me things. He showed me how, with hammer and cold chisel, so to shape the mouth of the squat N.B. firing shovels that they became tools to conjure with.

He taught me how to cut a gauge glass to size with a file, and make it as steam tight as a bottle, with cotton wick and the skin of the packing he used on the slide valve rods. Every day a job must be done, without depending on fitters to dry-nurse you. "Andra" Manzie was possibly a first class engineer without knowing it; there was not

12

a running repair he could not tackle and make *a* perfect job of.

I was lucky enough to have him fire my imagination and make me take the steps I did later to put something "under my hat" regarding steam engineering. He was a natural engineman, and even on this lowly job had the touch of the artist in his handling of the engine. From him I learned the knack of split-second timing, which is the secret of good shunting, but above all he was the first person who gave me encouragement to believe that you needn't be *a* Samson to become an engineman—but *he didn't know it.*

"Andra's" method of teaching was nothing if not direct. "Get doon into the hole," he would order, and I would step down to the iron floor of No. 39, on which level was the square aperture of the coal bunker facing the fire hole door, with about three feet of space to work in. "Now," Andra would direct, "don't fill the shovel as full as it will hold; just a wee drappie, laddie, and let's see ye land it in the faur awa' corner." And as we clattered and banged up and down "Andra" was giving me the "gen" on a subject on which some few years ago the British Railways issued a book, and made a film. They called it "Controlled Firing."

With no space in which to work it was possibly the best introduction to firing a locomotive anyone could have received, but above all, so far as I was concerned it swept away some of the fear which had been bred in my mind, even if I had put up a bouncing front to my "God in the bowler hat"—Jim Lawrie. For truth to tell, I was mortally afraid that he might prove right. If for nothing else than giving me reassurance on this, Andrew Manzie earned my undying gratitude; and when I fired to him regularly I nearly killed myself to show my gratitude. Andra never knew that, but it's true, just as true as the fact that my purgatory with the grease tin and "Shorty" came to a quite unexpected end.

I must have been something like a full nine months in Haymarket yard, and had made up my mind that I was there "for keeps" when someone mentioned casually that my service entitled me to a free pass anywhere on the North British system. I wouldn't believe it at first for in those days the word "entitled" wasn't part of a youngster's vocabulary. He wasn't "entitled" to anything so far as my experience had gone. He did what he was told, and maybe by the gracious benevolence of his betters he would be "privileged" to some casual notice. Hence I doubted my *right* to a free pass once a year, but it turned out that it was true and I grabbed at it.

Of course there were no frills attached to the pass, no holidays to spend in abandoned idleness. *Not one day in the year;* but what one has never had one doesn't grieve over, and this free ticket was manna from heaven, even if I had to get up at three on a Sunday morning to savour its full enjoyment, by taking the longest trip I could possibly make free, gratis and for nothing, to Aberdeen from Edinburgh.

The fact that I had to walk four miles to the station was a mere bagatelle. I was used to nothing else, even if there were horse trams running the streets of Edinburgh. Boys were seldom indulged in such pampered and expensive nonsense even with the fares as low as a halfpenny. So visualise me, pockets stuffed with gargantuan sandwiches, standing in the corridor of the "early Aberdeen" as near the engine as I could get, all ready to learn the road to Aberdeen, all tensed up to actually be on a trip behind *Dunedin,* N.B. Atlantic No. 874. At last I was going to experience what this fabulous journey was like, and just to give a line on how important a moment that was to me it has to be remembered that my journeys in passenger trains prior to this were limited to an occasional five miles or so on a Sunday School trip.

Since that day I've slogged through the swamps of East Africa, crossed the Persian Hills from Iraq to the Caspian Sea, travelled over the Himalayas to Deolali, and penetrated into most of the corners where my kind like to wander on the Continent of Europe, but it's true to say that in all my wanderings I've yet to get the thrill of that first trip to Aberdeen—even though I stood all the way there and back. Most of the way my head was poked outside looking for signals. If the safe conduct of that train had really depended on my vigilance I couldn't have been more earnest. The fact that my eyes, and ears, to say nothing of the back of my neck, collected their quota of smokebox ashes, mattered little—I "drove" that train in everything but reality. For three and a half glorious hours to Aberdeen and the same back, I had the time of my life, with an interlude at Aberdeen where I wolfed my sandwiches and washed them down with a penny bottle of lemonade (a third of my total capital this cost me), sitting watching the engines working in the stations. I think I must have been one of the pioneer loco-spotters of my generation.

When I arrived home at 9.15 that night I had had exactly three hours sleep out of the twenty-four, yet you wouldn't have believed it if you had seen me sprinting down the road thirty minutes after I got home, for awaiting me was a telegraph form on which was scribbled: "McKillop. Turn out on the cleaning 10pm" Here it was at last! "Big Jim" hadn't forgotten me after all. "Shorty," "yellow butt" and all it meant were behind me: I was on my way.

So I was one huge grin—which disappeared like a snowflake on a red hot stove when "Keekum Hislop," the night-shift gaffer, jerked a thumb and in laconic greeting said: " Jist report to Bloomfield, Norman, he's got a few fireboxes he wants to show ye." And Jack Bloomfield the boilersmith certainly had.

For ten solid hours (if you except two short breaks for eating, while my shirt was drying at the washing-out boiler fire) I cleaned the ashes from the top of the brick arches in innumerable fireboxes, and if you haven't been in a locomotive firebox it's easy enough to visualise what it's like if you put your hand inside the kitchen oven when the milder form of baking is in progress. Just to make it a little bit harder, like the brick in the boxer's glove, my labours were illuminated by a paraffin torch lamp that would have smoked out a badger. "Big Jim" was certainly taking me at my word. This was the hardest job a cleaner tackled in my young days: this, and building brick arches, to which I eventually graduated.

If this was a yarn in the true tradition, I should work in a little colour here on gritting my teeth, taking it on the chin and all that, but this wouldn't be true. It would read better if I could say something about "sweat begrimed toiling," but there was little perspiration possible from the gristle and bone which was me. Besides, I had taken steps to tackle this sort of thing, but that's another story.

So I built brick arches with a fair degree of success, "fair" being a relative term. A brick arch is supposed to spread the hot gases inside the firebox so that all the boiler tubes get their fair share of the heat to raise steam from the surrounding water. Nowadays the brick arch is erected in a comparatively short time by specially shaped fire bricks which fit meticulously, but when I was building them they were built of ordinary bricks with a wedge-shaped specimen to hammer in as a keystone to the arch. Naturally it was a hit or a miss, and I'm afraid my early efforts were in the "miss" category—until I got the brilliant idea which earned me my second threat of the sack.

My big worry on this job was to get the blessed things to stay put. More often than not my brick arches were lying on top of the fire before the engines were far on the road, and putting it mildly, I was not popular with the drivers of these engines. I lost a lot of sleep pondering the problem until one night I read something about glass in one of the textbooks which by now were my idea of light literature. It mentioned the degrees of heat necessary to melt glass—and I had my brain wave.

I collected all the broken bottles I could lay hands on and filled the gaps between the bricks of my firebox arches with glass—not merely here and there, but with thorough-going attention to every conceivable crevice. There were no more "fallen arches" after that. Instead, the darned things became a solid part of the firebox—and "Big Jim" was not amused; neither was I as I sighed my way out of his office.

But let's draw a veil over my good intentions. I learned the hard way that brick arches are made of bricks so that they can be taken down occasionally. If a locomotive designer wanted an arch permanently in position he would have welded it there, much as I had presumably done with my broken bottles.

Of the actual cleaning of engines I did little or nothing. I spent most of my "cleaning" service either with the boilersmith or in the fitting shop, where in the fashion of these times an amateur was allowed more scope than he is today. Actually I was rather enjoying myself. Glimmers of light were penetrating, for while it wasn't always easy to follow the textbook, it became simplicity itself when you manhandled the locomotive bits and pieces on the bench.

Here or hereabouts a great truth dawned. "Big Jim," in trying to cure my "engine phobia," had really increased the disease so that by the time I was considered "a real man" and fit to pass out as a fireman, I was more determined than ever to make the grade. I had a long way to go, but the first real step was taken when I was *invited* into the office of Mr. James Lawrie, Locomotive Foreman, Haymarket Shed and, with him grinning all over, was put through the test which made me a fireman on the North British Railway.

II

Cleaning to Kill

To become a fireman nowadays is almost like a State occasion compared with the simplicities of the test which placed me as the junior member on the footplate of a railway engine. Nowadays, doctors, superintendents, inspectors, clerks, all in their different spheres, are necessary to an engine-man's promotion. Forms and literature in prodigal quantities litter his path. Rules, regulations, notices, and appendices to the same, are like the leaves in the forest. He is docketed, recorded, and his promotional path generally supervised to an extent which make my up-gradings a pale thing indeed.

If a present-day Motive Power Superintendent had witnessed my examination to pass as a fireman he would have swooned in horror. Nowadays there are a lot of preliminaries before a cleaner is appointed to fireman. An inspector puts him through the grid on a multiplicity of rules, then gives him a mild grilling on steam generation, and the means thereto, as incorporated in locomotive design. And before all this a firing instructor has possibly given him the once-over and a whole lot of training to fit him for the life ahead. Thus have we advanced.

The examination to decide my fate on the footplate was nothing so ornate. I had never heard of, far less been examined by, a railway doctor. Nor was there any pandering by a benevolent inspector to my passionate thirst for locomotive knowledge. Had such an official as a firing instructor existed in the barren desert where I quested for information, I am afraid the poor chap would have had a pretty thin time. I would have fastened on him like a vampire until I'd sucked him dry of "gen". Come to think of it, I must have been a real menace to anyone who would talk "locomotive" to me.

No! there weren't many frills to being made a fireman in 1911— it mostly depended on how you looked. You had to *look* strong— and the bigger you were, the better chance you had of passing—*that and a good memory to enable you to pass the eyesight test.*

For, believe it or not, this test to me depended more on memory than it did on good eyesight. Maybe, however, that was my personal view, for providence had provided me with eyes, which, while they possibly failed to mirror my soul, served me reasonably well in seeing things properly. So I was disturbed very little when

I entered "Big Jim's" rather gloomy little office, was told to stand against the wall, and with a hand covering each eye in turn, was invited to tell the number of "dots" on a nine by two-and-a-half-inch white background.

The "dots" were little black squares about an eighth of an inch in size, and could be uncovered by a slide to any number up to about three dozen. As the "dots" were staggered all over the white surface I found it extremely difficult to *remember* whether I'd counted certain dots twice or not, and as I've said, it was quite a feat of memory to keep tab on them and get the correct number, quite apart from the fact that to this day counting bores me stiff.

I was lucky. I hit on the number each time the slide jigged over the dots and came to rest. I remember that I thought darkly that "Big Jim" was trying to see how fast he could make me count. This was pure biased fantasy, of course, but it must be admitted that rightly or wrongly my gaffer had rather got under my skin.

After the dots came a colour vision test. The present-day examination is done by the Edridge-Green lamp, an apparatus which displays small illuminated circles of colour which have to be named. My test was a far more simple affair, though I turned it, I'll swear, into one of the most complicated discussions "Big Jim" had ever encountered.

On the gaffer's table was a frame on which a two-foot wire was stretched and on the wire something like fifteen to twenty hanks of different coloured wool hung in foot lengths. On the table was a similar number of skeins. The test consisted of lifting a length of wool, placing it against a similarly coloured length hanging from the wire, and naming the colour correctly.

I approached this part of the ordeal with the utmost *sang froid;* once past the memory test of the much-to-be-feared "dots," the rest had no terrors for me, and in any case I was itching to get one back on "Big Jim." So, instead, of simply lifting a hank of wool and mumbling "red" or "green" or "pink," I stood as if fascinated, studying them closely.

"This one," I pronounced, "could be called salmon pink. I'm not quite sure of the particular shade but it's definitely pink I would say. This one" (I lifted another) "might be 'lime'." Here I pondered long enough to gaze at "Big Jim's" bulging eyes, and then continued brightly: "of course, it could be 'green', but then so much handling and exposure has made a difference, don't you think?"

Then I went along the complete line, pausing to embroil my gaffer in discussions on the infinite variety of shades I had picked up from listening to my sisters' gossip on dress materials. "Big Jim," as I well knew, couldn't care less about fine shades of red, green, and yellow, and to have a cleaner involving him in exotic terms such as "tangerine," "crushed strawberry" and the like, must have been a new and exasperating experience. To me, little devil that I was, it was highly satisfactory and wiped out of my system a little of the fireboxes which had bulked so largely in my young life up to then.

It was the same with the reading test. This was designed to see if an examinee was literate, and consisted of reading from the rule book. This was easy, but I wasn't going to have it that way and gravely invited Jim Lawrie to decide for me whether a comma should be this side of the "and" or the other side. And he couldn't have cared less.

But above all I went to town when we became locked in the intricacies of steam generation. Not that my gaffer wanted any such thing. Normally it was a simple matter of a short question or two, with an equally short answer, and then the examination was all over. But I was bursting to show off.

Don't forget I had practically lived in fire-boxes for months; not only that, but I had been reading textbooks and I went into the clinch with gay abandon.

"Steam generation? Oh, yes." I fairly licked my lips as I turned on the flow. "Convection currents," "gaseous vapour," "local expansion and contraction" all came tripping off my tongue with "Big Jim" looking at me with increasing horror and his eyes plainly asking what kind of freak had been unleashed upon him as, like Tennyson's brook, I went on and on.

"For heaven's sake stop!" he said at last. "If you can *make steam as fast* as you can blether, some day you'll maybe be a fireman. Start on the Haymarket pilot on Monday morning and we'll see if you're as good at working as you are at talking."

And that was that. I was a fireman; and right now before I go on with Andrew Manzie to fire saddle tank No. 39 I would like to "jump the gun" a little on a final note about "Big Jim."

I was only under him for three years, but I learned to know him well, and when I got more sense, I recognised him for the kindliest of souls who not only knew, but took the keenest of interest in the welfare of every man and boy in Haymarket. It was this same interest which had made him try and cure my foolishness (as he thought) respecting a career on the footplate. When I said good-bye to him in 1914 before leaving for war service abroad, he recalled his efforts to get me to give up, for he had really feared the hard life would beat me. I can still recall his parting words.

"I suppose this is another of your daft pig-headed notions," he said, referring to my joining-up. "You don't *have* to go, you know, but good luck, Norman; if you stick it the way you did your first year at Haymarket, there's no fear of you."

Since that day I've had on occasion some heart-warming things said to me, but few of them ever achieved the value or were treasured so long in my memory as that gruff, brief farewell, from James Lawrie, my first gaffer.

But let's get back to that "pug" in Haymarket goods yard.

No. 39, North British 0-6-0 "Saddle-back" tank engine, was almost clinical in its dazzling splendour; somehow it gave you the impression you get when you enter a hospital—almost *too* clean. This passion for the state akin to godliness nearly landed me into a hospital at the best, or the mortuary at the worst, on the very first day I joined Andrew Manzie as his regular mate.

Andrew had a rigid schedule for each day's work by the fireman, and Monday was the day set aside for polishing every bit of steel and brass in the cabless space we occupied on 39. I wanted to show "Andra" how grateful I was for past favours. Not only that, but there was keen rivalry amongst the firemen as to who could outshine the other in the matter of "spit and polish," so it's possible that what follows might have been due to my young and cocky desire to "show em' summat."

To fully understand it's necessary for those not au *fait* with polishing *hot* brass to know that this job is far removed from that practised domestically. There's no shaking a little liquid out of a nice wee tin on to a cloth and a final swift rub with a duster. That sort of thing was no good on 39, where most of the brass and copper fittings were sizzling hot—so hot that it would lift the skin off any unwary hand that touched these fittings.

Exposed to the elements, the brass was not only hot, but the stains from exposure were burned on, and this needed real hard work once a week to turn it into all the colours of the rainbow by means of ground bathbrick and a mixture of oils. If the brass-work was hot that day, the weather did nothing to cool it down. It was a sweltering summer's day, and for hours I was more or less "in the hole" scouring for dear life at gauge columns, throttle handle, reversing lever and flame plate.

Suddenly I felt queer and light-headed, and decided a spell on the "dicky" seat away from the heat was indicated. Whether I ever reached that seat I don't know, but I do know that the belt I received by hitting a wagon as I fell in a dead faint must have brought me back to sensible things and, the first sensible thing, as I remember, was to disentangle myself from a slowly moving coupling rod before it jammed me under the framing as 39 propelled a lift of coal wagons into a siding.

What followed really needs a psychiatrist to analyse it. I was up the steps of the engine like a shot and sitting on the dicky seat with butterflies going like mad in my stomach. I was agitated, not because I had nearly been killed, but in the hope that my driver hadn't noticed this exhibition of what I imagined was physical weakness. Providence was kind. "Andra" had his eyes fixed on the shunter, and if he did notice my absence, must have taken it for granted that I had nipped off to retrieve something which I had dropped, for he never even commented—and neither did I.

For a week after that the sales of embrocation went up. I was black and blue from shoulders to toe nails, but not even my mother knew how near her son had come to a sticky end, although by-and-large she was a long suffering victim of my railway back-chat.

Possibly to this adventure can be traced the interest I have always taken in the youngsters who came my way, for it drove into my skull something more than the pain from the bruise which outwardly adorned it for days afterwards. It made me realise that young enthusiasm can often lead to harm and that a tough, experienced engineman can quite well be unaware that what is easy to him isn't so easy to a lad not yet fully hardened.

My drivers were hardened physically all right. Andrew Manzie had a frame like a rock. His firing had been done to drivers who started their careers away back in the first days of the Edinburgh & Glasgow Railway in 1842, and whose mental approach to their engine was fashioned on the traditional methods of those whom George Stephenson himself, father of their craft, had trained. To "Andra" and his compeers the driving and firing of railway locomotives was a cult, not a job. It was something to be approached with measured reverence—not unlike the rigid ceremonial incorporated in the

Brigade of Guards, where one does not "go" but "proceeds"; and that procedure had to be done with unhurried, orderly efficiency, so far as the fireman was concerned. Maybe, too, the term "fireman" is slightly misleading for on 39, firing turned out to be the least of my duties.

I cleaned and cleaned and cleaned my engine. I cleaned her when she was standing (which was seldom); I cleaned her when she was moving (which was almost perpetually); I cleaned her in the sunshine, the rain, and the snow. I cleaned that engine and all that was on and in her, until I can recall to this day every bolt, nut, and pin which held her together. And the drill for all this made the laws of the Medes and Persians look like a pale set of half-baked exhortations.

For instance there was the matter of the ground bathbrick and the flax which was the preliminary to my death-defying dive. No modern fireman has ever seen this same flax-and-bathbrick act as performed by my generation. The colour and constituent of the flax was not unlike a swathe from Diana Dors' golden tresses. You cast this round the handbrake handle and plaited both loose ends, leaving a generous unplaited part about nine inches long in the centre.

Next (after firing enough coal to keep the engine going for a bit), you ground the bathbrick in the firing shovel, with a hammer which looked as if the head was silver-plated, but wasn't. When I had ground the bathbrick to what I thought was powder form, "Andra" tested a pinch of it between finger and thumb and pronounced: "That's no' fine enough, laddie, gie it another twenty meenits' or so." And I ground away at it until I'm sure Diana herself could have used it without danger to her superb complexion.

This done, there was the delicate operation of blending the bathbrick into a paste with oil—simple you might think; but you don't know the lads of the 1900's, for each engineman had his own pet theories regarding the oil which would produce the most dazzling array of colours on the hot brass. In "Andra's" case it was a blending of rape oil, engine lubricating oil and a spot of paraffin, as carefully measured as a most meticulous chemical formula.

Nor was any kind of sloppy mess allowed to emerge from the formula. The oil and bathbrick must so combine that it almost became one in a smooth paste, which nevertheless carried sufficient "bite" to lift off the stains and at the same time clean the brass when applied by the fibrous flax pig-tail. The next step was to polish with a duster (usually pinched from the domestic store) and then finish off with old newspapers (also of domestic origin).

That rather long-winded example of an ordinary "chore" on 39 perhaps illustrates better than anything why I had to spend so much time "in the hole" with the hot fire on my legs, the quite unprotected boiler-end roasting the rest of me in front, and the sun with almost tropical force attending to the back of my neck. If I hadn't fainted, it's quite possible I'd have melted, so determined was I to "show 'em."

That was only one part of the drill on "39." Each day besides cleaning the outside of the engine from stem to stern, I had a special job to do. The gauge lamp and the two headlamps had all to be scoured inside until they put ordinary silver to shame. It was the same with the handrails and smoke-box steel fittings. The safety valves, whistle and the brass cylinder oil cups on the smoke-box had to *glitter,* while the outside footplate, side-rods and buffers received special treatment every day. First they were washed with paraffin and water, then they got a course of beauty treatment from the flax and bathbrick then they were washed with paraffin and finally rubbed over with tallow.

This latter job was about the only one which could not be done when 39 was shunting and I earned a pan of praise from "Andra" for developing a split-second technique of anticipating the train's coming into the yard, having the fire in order and then spending every moment while we waited to couple to the trains in feverish activity on the bits I couldn't clean when moving.

I also developed an agility which would have filled a certain scientist's heart with gratified satisfaction as proof that man was descended from the monkey. If the present Board of Trade had seen me perched on the handrail with no other visible means of support, cleaning the saddle-tank while 39 dashed back and forth, they would either have put me in a padded cell, or alternatively have incarcerated the directors of the N.B.R. for allowing such flagrant disregard of the rules for safe working on the railways.

But rules or no rules, I was happy. I was learning my craft even if nowadays it's done in a slightly different way. In fact, apart from the fundamental technique, there's quite a lot the engineman doesn't do now which were *musts* when I fired to "Andra" Manzie.

Today every shunting pilot stops for twenty minutes during the eight-hour shift to allow the enginemen to take their food. In 1911, with a ten-hour day newly introduced on the N.B.R. and with the "Caley" still working eleven hours as a shift, there was no provision made for taking one's "piece." Mostly the mealtime was regulated by the flow of traffic or the goodwill of the shunters, who, if they were too busy, would nip into the "bothy" one at a time for a quick "bite" while the other one kept the pilot going.

But once every twenty-four hours the fire of 39 *had* to be cleaned, and for this we had thirty minutes. Thirty minutes isn't a long time when a firebox full to the "gunnel" has to be emptied via the fire-hole door in single shovelfuls. But here again it was no mere clattering or aimless throwing out. "Andra" saw to that. Each shovelful had to be extracted so carefully that not an ash must drop on the floor, and then the eight-foot long iron clinker shovel had to be manipulated over the side on which the wind would blow the fine ash dust away from the engine.

Have you ever tried to wangle a heavy iron shovel measuring eight feet in a confined space which had restricted areas measuring no more than three or four feet? To clean the fire of 39 was equal to a practical session with Euclid in one of his more difficult moods. And 39 wasn't the worst one by a long chalk.

It wouldn't have been so bad if the thirty minutes was utilised for this alone, but there were sandboxes to fill, and occasionally coal to take aboard. That was the fireman's part of the job, but while I was doing this my mate was imitating the busy bee, if "Andra" could ever be likened to a bee. He oiled the engine and each day performed some sort of job which nowadays is as dead as the dodo.

For instance there were glands to pack. This was the era before metallic packing was used to make the piston and valve rods steamtight. The drivers attended to this themselves, and if you had seen those piston rods, and watched the engine working in steamtight perfection, it might make you ponder on the advances *(sic)* we have made since those good old days *(sic* again). I'm very much aware that in some respects the "good old days" weren't so good, and maybe some day I will give chapter and verse, but in this book I'm concerned with *real* enginemen, and there's no doubt about it—these old hands were good.

Andrew Manzie, like most others of his breed, had a most complete set of tools. Some of these he had made himself, and it was a routine job for him to attend to his big ends, small ends, and coupling rods in every respect, short of dismantling them for stripping or renewal of the bearing brasses.

It was routine to "Andra" to renew trimmings, pack injector steam keys and other such jobs on 39—all quite legitimate "repairs" which are now booked for a fitter to carry out. Nowadays it's the rule rather than the exception to see blows of steam whenever a railway engine or a part of the apparatus is moved. In 1911 I heard "Big Jim" threaten to take a driver off the footplate for "gross carelessness"—his description of a blow of steam through a piston gland, caused by a slight cording of the piston rod by bad packing and lack of lubrication.

If "Andra" was decent to me as a young greaser he was even more so when I fired for him, for he inveigled (how I do not know) a bunch of cleaners to assist me to "dodge the column." He insisted I should learn to clean a fire properly, but once I satisfied him I could do so, three or four cleaners came regularly to do the job and fill the sandboxes—while I worked with "Andra."

He taught me how to make a four-strand plait with cotton torch lamp wick to act as "shangies" or "weasies" on the piston and valve rods, so that they got the full benefit of the oil dropping from the pipe above them. A four-strand plait is flat and fits the gland nuts more snugly than a three-strand one. He could perform wonders with copper wire and worsted in the making of oil trimmings, and it was an improvement on some of his ideas in this respect which brought me an official "pat on the back" many years later when, as a driver, I conducted a three months' trial on lubrication.

Even at the risk of boring the non-technical I've expanded a little on this theme, because I'm inclined to think that it is being forgotten that there was more than merely "driving" to the old-timers. Maybe that is why I like the term "engineman" rather than "driver." There's a whale of a difference, if you know what I mean.

Not that "Andra" Mamie couldn't *drive* engines. He could do that all right, but what was more important to me was that he insisted that I must drive too—maybe as a reward for lying flat on my stomach screwing up the top nuts of piston glands, while he was underneath doing the same to the bottom nuts, both of us screwing each half turn as exactly as if to do otherwise would bring the heavens down upon us, when all that was at stake was a minute puff of steam from a gland not absolutely "square on."

"Andra" started my driving lessons with the light engine on our daily run of two hundred yards or so to the shed for our thirty minutes' engine duties. He made me experiment with the throttle and steam brake until I'd got the "feel" of the engine. The first day this happened I went about bragging to the younger fry—not openly, of course, just a casual "I brought her up to the shed myself this morning." But was I proud, and you can say that as often as you like.

Our engine was considered very modern and was really powerful. Once I had mastered the knack of lifting empty wagons without too much snatch, and manipulating the throttle so that once the couplings were tight I kept them that way until the brake was used to stop. "Andra" started to initiate me into the finer points of classic shunting. Don't ever believe that this type of job is just plain see-sawing back and forth. There are more varieties of movement in one mixed lift of wagons than there is in the famous "57" of sauce and bean fame, and I gained a fair knowledge of most of them under my mate's tuition.

He would glance from his perch on the seat opposite and warn me: "Now watch that coal in the middle o' that lift!" And I would open the throttle an infinitesimal fraction and shut it as the first coupling tightened and the second one started to extend. So it would go on until some hundred yards away that heavy mass in the centre brought movement almost to a stand.

The trick then was to gauge just the amount of steam needed to keep everything moving so gently that each heavy wagon was lifted without a jerk until everything was on the move. That was the moment you gave her "the works" and laid the throttle wide open to race like mad up the shunt until, with the throttle closed once more, the steam brake came into action with a gentle hiss, bringing all the buffers together. Then, just as ruthlessly as you had treated the throttle, you "nicked" the brake handle full on, and waited for the psychological moment to reverse.

This moment was important. If you did not reverse the lever, work the brake, and throttle to start moving back at the correct moment one of two things happened. If you were too quick the wheels of the engine locked and she would slide like a sledge, with a danger of wearing a flat on the engine tyres. If you were a second too slow, that mass of coal would rebound like a shot out of a gun—and if you heard such a "shot" you didn't need to be told it was the noise from a broken coupling. Providence had to be kind to any fireman who did that when driving to Andrew Manzie.

I never broke a coupling when on with him, but I experienced his displeasure once—and once was enough. It was the lubricator that did it. There were no sight feed or mechanical lubricators on the shunting "pugs" in 1911. To oil the valves there was a cup on the storm board, and the drill to get oil through the delivery pipe to the valves was to pour it into the cup when the engine was running with the throttle closed. The oil was sucked in, the oilway was closed, then a key turned which sent a jet of steam along the pipe to carry the oil to its destination.

One day while my mate was at this, I was busy watching the shunters, and opened the throttle just as Andrew was in the act of pouring oil into the open cup. Whewl that did it. A miniature "gusher" of hot oil erupted with a noise like an angry snake, and never again do I wish to hear the blast of sound which shivered the very clouds above us as Andrew gave tongue—and it didn't stop at sound.

In one violent grab he yanked me off the driving seat and cast me into my corner as if I was a bundle of dirty cotton waste. I spent the remainder of the shift using plenty of that material to clean not only the engine, but Andrew as well. Even his moustache was like an oily rag.

III
Lodging Turn—Old Style

Andrew Manzie and "pug" 39, along with a few other shunting pilots and their drivers, were eventually left behind in my march of progress. I must confess that while I regretted leaving the company of my mates I wasn't at all sorry to leave the pilots. My eyes were forever fixed on the then top speed limits, an awesome sixty miles an hour. At least, it was awesome to me.

So while I picked up an immense amount of locomotive lore, the lower bracket firing jobs passed without incident—that is, if you except the clipping of "Hookey" Walker under the chin, or rather on the beard under which the chin hid. Quite a spontaneous performance that was, without premeditation, and, I hope, undue malice.

"Hookey" drove a wee 0-4-0 pilot which must have been first-cousin to Stephenson's *Rocket*. It meandered back and forth in a goods yard, each shunt a painful wheezing tottering adventure, and at the end of each shunt I was frenziedly twirling the hand brake trying to stop its ten-mile-an-hour progress. There was no other means except the reversing lever of stopping the thing.

I wasn't a giant yet I towered above the tiny boiler end, and quite frankly hated the thing. To me it wasn't an engine at all and what made it worse was the fact that the place where it shunted was near where I stayed, and I quite seriously dreaded some of my non-railway pals seeing me on this apology for a locomotive, after the way I used to "blow" to them. In conversation I rarely mentioned anything smaller than an N.B. Atlantic.

Maybe this (if the truth must be told) had some bearing on the punch I landed on "Hookey's" chin, but the direct reason was his peculiar sense of humour, of which I was totally unaware. He thought it the height of fun to nip his fireman when he was bending. The first time he did it to me was the last, for I reacted quite naturally to the training I had been receiving from no less a person than Tancy Lee himself—and if you don't know who "Tancy" was, he was the bloke who once beat Jimmy Wilde, one of Britain's best ever flyweights.

There's a lot behind that story other than a punch on a sadistically inclined humourist's chin—a lot which has no place in this yarn, except the fact that when I realised Jim Lawrie had decided to try me out, I took measures to toughen myself to stand all the hot fireboxes into which he cared to shove me. Boxing was part of the toughening process.

Then I met Jack Harding and a Drummond 0-6-0 tender goods engine. Jack took an almost embarrassing interest in me and my ideas. He was definitely interested in both of my phobias—especially the toughening process. Six feet of bone, muscle and gristle, with a head which wouldn't have disgraced a statue of the classical Greek athlete, Jack was a champion wrestler in his native Cumberland. Cumberland and Westmorland wrestling isn't like the catch-as-catch-can or the modern all-in stuff. I should know, for Jack, believe it or not, thought I was a good subject to practise on—you'll observe I said practise "on" not "with". But I laid down a condition for this unofficial duty on a fireman's part. In return for wrestling, I was to be allowed to *drive* the engine occasionally and he would fire it. And so it was agreed.

So I drove that engine under the Forth Bridge, and across it. I oiled it, packed the glands, shunted interminably at almost every siding and generally had the time of my life. Jack had a magnificent way with a shovel, but best of all he could manage the reversing lever as if it was a toy—which quite often it wasn't.

The reversing lever was a sore point with me on this particular engine. It was, contrary to the usual practice, on the fireman's side of the cab, and if you've ever had a ten hours spell reversing a slide valve engine you'll know why I made that bargain with Jack Harding. If you left even a dribble of steam pressing on the huge area of the slide valves it was real hard work to operate that reverser, but Jack never seemed to notice, for he yanked it back and forward with apparent ease, and only one hand.

Each day I allowed Jack to practise his Cumberland and Westmorland technique on me while we waited for a lift of oil tanks at a shale mine. You've no idea how we worked to arrive at that mine, well ahead of the time the tanks would be ready. The "wrestling" took place on a grassy triangle, where I'd brace my feet and legs in the approved manner, catch hold of a short length of rope (a concession, this, to the fact that I couldn't reach round Jack's waist) then hang on like grim death while Jack tossed the legs from under me, solemnly intoning "Cross-buttock," or "Flying Mare," or some such wrestling jargon.

So far as I can recollect this performance consisted mainly of having my ribs nearly crushed in, being folded up like a jack-knife, and ending up with my shoulders bashing the turf with such goodwill that I'll swear there's a permanent hollow in that spot to this day. Jack enjoyed it all thoroughly, except for one occasion when I turned my text book studies to good account. It was old Archimedes who gave me the hint. You know the bit about the law of leverage — "give me a fulcrum point and I will move the world." As usual almost everything I thought up had to have some bearing on locomotives and it was in reading about the leverage points in the braking system that it suddenly dawned on me it could be handy in wrestling.

So I watched Jack's feet instead of gazing into space and one never-to-beforgotten moment I slipped *my* buttock into *his* waistline and put the Archimedes formula to practical use. Admittedly, I did it only once; but what a glorious feeling that was, quite apart from the important fact that it opened a new vista—the easy way to do hard firing.

For it is true that this locomotive game, so far as the physical effort is concerned, can be reduced to a streamlined rhythm of which little is said even nowadays, either in the instruction books or by those who have the tutoring of the youngsters who come into the grade. Personally I never omitted this angle when preaching my locomotive gospel to the hundreds of lads I have trained, and I'm willing to bet it helped more than a few of them to a more enjoyable life on the footplate than they might otherwise have had.

Make no mistake about the firing I did do to Jack Harding. Even if it was a comparatively small engine it was hard enough for me as we ran one of our trips a mere twenty miles or so in distance. It was hard because Jack, by the very nature of his make-up, was no exponent of the finer shades in locomotive operation. When he shoved a throttle open it was *wide-open,* with no fiddling with slender cut-offs, and maybe it was necessary on gradients of 1 in 70. Whether it was necessary or not, the fact remains that those engines, when working heavily, could pour a chimney-thick spume of living fire sky-high, and no engine can do this without a pretty busy fireman in the cab.

I never bothered about Jack and his gay bashing. I packed the firebox and kept on packing 'em in, and Jack kept the fire dancing. We were never short of steam, and certainly knew that we had two injectors in working order, for we needed them on this particular night run to Townhill, one of the trips on which Jack absolutely refused to allow me to drive. We had a full load of whisky on that run, and as he remarked: "Whisky's too precious, my lad, to allow you to monkey about with the throttle … you stick to coal wagons. You can break them to your heart's content."

I learned most everything about freight train working from Jack Harding in the happiest way. In fact, our contact assumed more than that normally enjoyed between driver and fireman. We became firm friends until the day of his death, and this friendship included his wife as well. The first time I made the acquaintance of Mrs. Harding was the sequel to a funny incident which had nothing to do with firing or driving a railway engine. It all arose because I taught Jack how to ride a bicycle. Not that the riding of the cycle was conceived in any spirit of hilarity. It was definitely not so, yet neither was it done for pleasure. Jack determined to "learn to cycle or bust," as an alternative to walking sixteen miles a day, or staying away from home for five days a week, or just getting the sack. The yarn is an interesting insight into the conditions of those days and may bear recounting.

The engine on which I fired to Jack Harding was one of two stationed a mere eight miles from our depot. When a driver or fireman was rostered for this job he merely received a note: "Book on at Ratho for Queensferry Goods." That was all: no nonsense about lodging allowances, travelling time, or any of the amenities enjoyed nowadays. You were expected to *stay* at Ratho, which for quite obvious reasons was out of the question to a married man with a wage of 30s. or a fireman with 20s. a week.

For years the practice had been for the drivers and firemen to travel by passenger train to Ratho and back. Jack and I did the same until we were asked for a ticket. We hadn't one because we couldn't afford it and that started something. We were informed in writing that "this practice must cease." We replied stating our case, and continued to travel by passenger train to Ratho. A second letter told us of the dire consequences of this flagrant disobedience, and a third letter informed us curtly that if we continued this practice we "would be instantly dismissed."

So we tried riding in goods trains, but this left us little time to sleep between shifts, quite apart from the fact that on most of our return trips we had to jump from the moving goods van, or be carried past our destination by twenty miles or so. This was dangerous too, as one night in the pitch dark we didn't notice that the surfacemen had laid heaps of ballast on our usually smooth "landing ground." We looked like a couple of Red Indians in their most fantastic war paint after that jump.

We decided then to walk it—rather a heroic decision, as we found. It was winter, and maybe I'm imagining when I say that even the Scottish winters are not what they were. Be that true or otherwise, I do know that Jack and I have walked no more than a hundred yards behind each other, and been unaware that we were doing so, because the snowfall was so heavy most of the mornings we walked those eight miles. By the time we had done this for a month or two, eight miles out and eight miles back at the end of the shift, we were a bit browned off, and quite evidently needed our sleep.

We gave in. We would lodge at Ratho—our way. We couldn't afford to pay for "digs" and our bright idea was to sleep on alternative nights in the old carriage which served the guards as a "booking-on" cabin. At least we would get a decent sleep on three out of six nights. But that was before we tried it out.

I brought plenty of food and books. Jack brought nothing at all. He made do with yards of steak bought in the village, fried on the firing shovel, and washed down with ale. Steak was sevenpence a pound, and ale twopence a quart bottle. We could have slept all right if the rats had kept quiet, but they seemed to be engaged on a systematic attempt to devour our abode. We came to the conclusion that after they had eaten the place they might start on us, so the next brilliant idea was born.

We would save up and buy second hand "bikes." Not cheap trash, something that would stand rough usage. We would spend at least 30s. and make sure of road-worthiness, reliability, and goodness knows how many other qualities we expected for our thirty-bob and strangely enough we got most of what we anticipated.

When Spring was near, and the roads clear of snow, we started on the great adventure. I could ride a bike, but Jack had never tried, so I spent a hectic fortnight in the quiet byways tutoring my driver in the act of Blondin. He was not only convinced that to balance on two wheels was an utter impossibility, but proved conclusively to his own satisfaction by trying to sit on the machine while it was stationary. It took me a good hour arguing with him before he would try balancing the bike while in motion, but once he got the first brief spot of motion on that bicycle he became so entranced with the idea that he completely forgot the immense power of his enormous leg muscles.

When he trod on the pedals I nearly had my arms jerked out of their sockets trying to hold him upright by the saddle standard. It was for all the world as if I was trying to hold back the engine we worked when the throttle was wide open. This wouldn't have been so bad if he hadn't quite happily ignored the possibility of steering, and the way he would sit transfixed, his legs pedalling furiously, driving straight at a dyke had me thinking occasionally that we'd have been better walking.

The inevitable was bound to happen. At the end of a fortnight Jack could more or less sit upright on a moving bicycle, miss the more obvious impediments to his flight, and in the wide-open spaces, I believe would have left anything else on the road standing still—that is, if there had been anything else there at 3 in the morning, which was our dayshift time of departure.

Our new system of transport lasted exactly three days. On the third day, coming home in broad daylight, Jack, with his eyes wide open, steered as straight as a die, and at speed, for a two feet-thick wall three miles from Edinburgh. The wall won.

I assisted him to gather the bits and pieces, and we walked home to tea in Jack's house, where Mrs. Harding told me that she couldn't have been more pleased at the sight of anything than that wrecked machine. "He's better and safer sticking to engines," was her verdict on a whole thirty shillings' worth "gone with the wind."

It may appear crazy to present-day enginemen that it never once entered our heads to "chuck the job." It may be considered an act of lunacy to go to such lengths merely to drive and fire a Drummond 0-6-0 on a small time goods train. Even to me at this moment writing about it, and trying to analyse the reason behind it all, it is extremely difficult to produce sense, or what most people would call sense.

Certainly the wages were no factor in binding one to a railway engine. The conditions imposed by those in authority were almost brutal in their rigid discipline, while the hours we worked round the clock were such that even in those days of long working hours they were considered abnormal. Had Jack or I been asked in 1912 why we did it, we wouldn't have had an answer. We didn't even think of "chucking in." We didn't even consider we were getting a bad "break." After writing that last sentence, the question naturally comes to mind: were we so dumb, or ignorant, or so mentally out of perspective that we didn't realise that the conditions we worked under were plainly not fair?

No, we were neither dumb nor ignorant: quite without cant I can say that. What really mattered to us was that we were *allowed* to handle a railway engine. Long hours, tough going, poor conditions of service and little pay had nothing to do with it. I firmly believe that if we could have afforded it, we would have driven and fired that Drummond 0-6-0 for nothing, and even today there are quite a number who are bitten the same way.

Not only on the footplate is this evident. Off-hand I could mention an eminent publisher; the head of a divinity college (now retired); a professor of engineering; and dozens of doctors, lawyers, and others in what Nancy Mitford describes as the "U" category, who at the drop of a hat would occupy the driving seat on a railway engine if officialdom opened its heart and invited them to "have a go."

The fact is, that driving and firing a steam railway engine is a perpetual challenge. It's not like driving a motor or any other form of transport. You become, if not actually part of it, as near that as doesn't matter. And this is true whether it's my Drummond or the biggest that runs the rails.

To an engineman it's all one, so long as he can feel the rise and fall of the trailing axleboxes under his feet, the strain of the drawbar under the load, the feeling of life in response to his hand on the regulator, and the sheer music of big ends, coupling rods, and steel-to-ringing-steel contact of driving wheels on the rail.

Maybe too, there's the fascination of proving oneself, an urge we all have more or less. For again even on my Drummond this was possible, and of course proving oneself is always an adventure. That it was possible to have adventure on this lowly "champering iron horse" was true, as I found in both firing and driving them, although I didn't call it by that romantic title when adventure came my way.

No, I took a pretty dim view of it, and while it lends savour to a yarn when looked at in perspective most of the incidents which happen on the footplate aren't welcomed. In point of fact, though it sounds paradoxical, it is true that while I was a hero-worshipper of engines I was all for a quiet life on the footplate. But sometimes I didn't get it that way. For instance …

One of the trips which Jack and I made was to an oil refinery mid-way up a mountain. It was a few miles of climb on gradients which, to say the least, were formidable. It wasn't the climb which bothered us, although that was tough enough, especially in the winter with rime, frost, and fallen leaves making the rails like glass. Our job was to climb that bank using as little sand as possible, as we needed all the sand we could carry for coming *down*. It was this return trip which introduced me to the first of quite a few experiences on a runaway train. It also showed me the calibre of the driver to whom I was firing.

As usual, when we started the descent the guard was "pinning down wagon brakes" and if you ever read the official drill for this performance you'll see that it involves the train being slowly set in motion, while the guard, with the aid of a "brake stick," forces the wagon brake handles down a slotted guide then pushes an iron pin through one of the numerous holes in the guide to hold the brake-blocks to the wheels. This goes on until the driver considers he has enough brake-power applied on the train to augment that of the engine for safe control down an incline. It has one disadvantage, however, once the wagon brakes are applied and the guard rejoins his van there is no means either of increasing or of decreasing the train brake-power, short of stopping and man-handling the wagon brakes individually.

That night we had used a lot of sand going up—it was either that or never reaching the refinery at all. We were keeping our fingers crossed as we slowly moved off down the bank and felt the gradual resistance as Sandy, the guard, pinned the brakes on the long train behind us. It was a nice problem for Jack Harding to decide. We were tender first, with no hope of getting sand to six out of the twelve wheels we had on the engine and tender with brake power, little sand in our front boxes to augment our back sanders on the brakes of the train behind us, and ahead rail conditions which, while unknown, were almost certain to resemble the surface of a skating rink.

"We'll try it," said Jack. I gave Sandy a wave with my gauge lamp, and watched his lamp as he stood by the lineside before mounting the van to give me the "green" that he was safely aboard. The train brakes were holding us to the extent that Jack still had the "steam on her face" to keep moving. Then the gradient took charge; at no more than ten miles an hour, I wound the tender hand brake handle as cautiously as if the blocks were precious china.

For a few turns of the tender wheels the click of the rail-joints told us the wheels were revolving. I turned the brake handle a mere quarter of a turn to offset the slightly rising speed as the weight of the train settled on our *wee* Drummond. The rail-joint clicks ceased. The tender wheels were skidding.

Nothing else for it! I released the brake a little, the clicks restarted, but the train speed was rising. Jack nodded at the back sand handle; I pulled it as he gently opened the steam to the power brake and for a few moments the speed decreased. "Try half-open," Jack suggested. I pushed the sand handle gently forward to about the three-quarter mark and we went into what I believe would now be called "a toboggan routine."

Those rails were certainly in no condition to grip a smooth set of wheel tyres, minus sand. We found this out in due course, when the sand stopped running, and the weight behind felt like a giant hand pushing us relentlessly and at increasing speed down the bank. Shortly, with both back and front sand handles in the full open position—a futile enough sign that they were empty—we started to rock-'n-roll.

"We're off," said Jack laconically, handing me a blank report sheet with one hand while he "jagged" the steam brake-handle with the other—off-on, off-on, off-on, with the wheels locking almost as soon as the brake-blocks touched them. "Write on that sheet and tie it round a bit of coal," he commanded. So I scrawled a shaky "Have run away, keep the junction clear" at Jack's dictation, and started a series of pop-whistles half a mile away from the next signalbox.

The signalman was on his toes alright, and jigged his lamp to let me see that he spotted the white object which landed near the box. The message was delivered. The Drummond to my imagination was now "hurtling," but Jack didn't seem to be unduly perturbed. "Here," he said, and pushed me into his corner, "keep on jagging I'm going to see about sand when we hit the level. Keep your eyes on me and when I give you the tip slam the brake on, and keep it on."

I "jagged" the brake handle in futile frustration as I kept my eyes glued to Jack's dim form crouching halfway along the footplate. In a minute he waved the gauge lamp, and I slapped that steam brake handle full on as the Drummond hit the start of that few hundred yards of level before she again accelerated down another long gradient to the junction.

The grind of the wheels on sand was music, the smell of heating brake-blocks the most beautiful aroma that had ever assailed my nostrils. But it was short-lived relief. We shot over the level like a flash, and were heading hellfor-leather down the bank again at speed. Jack worked his way round the smoke-box to the other side and I couldn't see him; I was "jagging" again like mad, for our wheels were once more skidding.

Suddenly something plucked at that Drummond as if it was a toy engine. The coupling "pinged" as the jerk nearly broke it, and I was bashed up against the boiler face like a stone from a catapult. I jumped across the cab to see how Jack had fared and caught a reassuring wave from the gauge lamp, so my blood pressure eased a bit. And so did the speed. The Drummond was no longer in control of the train. It was the train brakes which were now doing the controlling as the sand on that level stretch behind us took effect. We slowed and slowed, and slowed, until without much effort on our part (if you accept sighs of relief from me) we halted, no more than a hundred yards from the outer home signal which protected the junction.

Jack was back in the cab before this happened, and was doing things with the brake handle, which showed up my quite mechanical and amateur efforts at "jag braking." So far as I could see he hadn't turned a hair, and the only remark he made to me as we stopped had nothing to do with a runaway train.

"Better wipe your nose, and get a fire in," he said.

It was only then I realised that I hadn't got off scotfree from that bash against the face-plate, and when I bent to shovel coal on the fire I felt the wet cold of the perspiration on my spine. Yes, I had the "wind-up" on that first experience on a runaway train. I just couldn't believe that this adventure was just another problem to be solved by my driver as if it all was in the day's work.

By the time we finished the shift I had it all lined up—what a yarn to tell the boys next day. That is, until Jack put my views in better perspective, which he did as we trudged home side by side that night.

"Where did you get that sand, Jack?" I asked. I was still puzzled about that act he had staged on the footplate. "Oh, there's always a wee drop of sand left in the bottom of the sand-boxes after it stops running," he replied. "All I did was push it down the hole." Then reflectively, as if he had missed something, he observed: "I used to do it regularly when I fired on these jobs."

Jack couldn't see my red face, but he must have sensed it in the long silence which followed, for he added, "I would have let you do it, but my arm is longer than yours." It might have deceived many, but didn't deceive me. Quickly I decided there was no yarn for the boys next day, or rather that the yarn should follow a different pattern, a pattern I'm pleased to record for the first time.

Jack Harding was a real guy. Under his rugged exterior was the gentlest of natures. I fired to him later when things happened on the engines of express trains, things which required quick action and resource, and maybe a bit of risk. It was always he who jumped to it, and saw that his fireman took the easy end of the stick. Yet, in his slow drawl he always made it appear that there was nothing he did which his fireman couldn't just as casually have accomplished.

To a skinny specimen like myself, to have Jack assure me that I had his strength, his experience, or his cool judgment, should have been funny, if I had been inclined to feel that way, but I admired him too greatly for that. He possibly put "sand" into me as well as on the rails that night we ran away, and I had need of that occasionally, in firing to others who were less sensitive to my feelings than Jack Harding.

IV

A Spare Life but a Gay One

The "five and six spare" was what its name implies. It was a link of drivers prepared to drive anything on any job whatever for a wage of five shillings and sixpence per ten-hour day. They were mostly young drivers who couldn't have suited me better if I'd had the job of picking them as mates, which of course I hadn't, otherwise I'd never have fired to "The Brute."

His name doesn't matter. "The Brute" is ample description, and he was hated by every one of my firing compeers. His huge moon face only altered to snarl, mostly at his fireman, whom he treated as the fount of all his troubles—which were many. I fired to him for an all-too-long brief period.

One of our jobs was to relieve two Atlantics and a "Scott" 4-4-0 off the Aberdeen and Montrose runs respectively, and to do this we walked to and from the depot to the station for each relief. This meant that the first two engines had to be stabled in the quickest of time (in those days "disposal men" hadn't been thought up).

To the rest of the drivers in the "five and six" link the turning, coaling, tank filling, fire cleaning and so-on, was a team job. To "The Brute" it merely meant a snarling, critical supervision of his sweating fireman. To get the meaning of what this entails you've got to realise that the stabling of an N.B. Atlantic was no kindergarten job.

Quite apart from man-handling the engine on the turntable, some eleven or twelve tons of coal had to be emptied and built on to the tenders. This was done from four-wheeled bogies, each of which held half a ton. There was no front "cage" on the Atlantic tenders then, so to accommodate the full supply of coal it was the practice to build a wall of lumps all round the tender and fill it up, streamlined and rounded at the top, so that it passed through the tunnels safely.

This "setting up" was a job which was normally done in company with the driver, and most of them were as expert as dry stone dykers are in the formation of rigid walls. "The Brute" merely stood and watched while I sweated and toiled, then did his best to knock down the wall with the firing shovel "to see if it was O.K." as he put it. Occasionally he succeeded in knocking a "setter" down, and this used to give him immense satisfaction, for it meant that delay took place, and his fireman had to run like a hare to the station to be in time for the next train he was to relieve.

The N.B. Atlantic was the only engine fitted with a drop grate, and for this I was truly thankful. The usual method was for the fireman to push the fire through the "dropped" part of the firebox, while the driver by means of a long "pricker" kept the opening clear. This was before the days of ash-pits. The fire was dropped on the ground between the rails, consequently it built up quickly if it wasn't cleared.

That didn't worry "The Brute" one bit. He cleared off to the fitting shop, where after you had jumped up and down clearing and pushing, cleaned out the smokebox, then lain flat on your stomach to clean the ashpan, you humbly sought your driver and informed him the engine was ready to stable in the shed.

Strangely enough I didn't mind his palming all the hard work on to me—rather did I revel in it, for I was getting tough physically each day of my young life. What I resented most was the way we walked between the depot and the station. I cannot at any time recall my walking with this man. I always walked behind him.

This to me was a bitter humiliation. I had placed a maybe too great value on the fact that my previous drivers had not been too exalted to "crack" with me on this and that concerning their engines. I tried once to enter into this *"flow of soul"* with "The Brute" and retired defeated. First he made it patently obvious that he knew little and cared less how a locomotive "ticked," but when I tried to mention the obvious simplicities which were the A.B.C. of this game I was so interested in, he merely snorted, and we resumed our single file progression.

Later he went to the foreman and said I was no good as a fireman, which, of course, in these days was the prelude to a sure dismissal. The reason? The reason is also the story of my first "cold run."

One of the trains we ran in this spare link was *The Tourist*. During the summer months it started somewhere in the South of England and it was our job to run it from Edinburgh to Perth. It wasn't a regular train and we normally got little warning that it was on the way. It left in the early hours of the morning from Waverley. Nobody liked working this non-stop express for the sole reason that it was vacuum brake-fitted. We were used to the Westinghouse brake, and it is true to say that the vacuum was not only disliked, but that the vacuum apparatus on the N.B. engines wasn't always as good as it is today. If it had been I might have had a better run, or maybe if "The Brute" had known more about it we might have got to Perth with less loss of time.

As it was we were handicapped from the start. The engine we had was the one relieved off the Montrose, a "saturated 'Scott'" called *Helen Macgregor*. It was a rush to get her ready, and the smokebox had never been cleaned. I knew before we left that this meant steam trouble.

But what worried me most was the antics of my driver with the vacuum apparatus in the cab. We hadn't gone a mile, when in spite of the injector working full-bore, the water started to come down steadily in the gauge glass. It was the use of the big vacuum injector which was taking that water out of the boiler, even if the engine was being flogged unmercifully from the start. What was happening is possibly hard to believe in this day of the universal use of the vacuum brake.

Normally the big ejector steam is used for a brief period to create the necessary vacuum in brake pipes and cylinders quickly. After that the small ejector is used to maintain the extraction of the air with a negligible volume of steam. Nowadays the big ejector isn't such a deadly drain on the boiler as was that "solid cone" one which was going full blast on *Helen Macgregor* that hectic morning on "The Tourist."

It was not in the nature of my mate to ease the lot of a fireman in trouble through lack of steam or water. As I looked across the cab about all I could see of him was his boots, as he hung outside looking for signals (he was that kind of driver). The water was coming lower and lower as we rocketed through Turnhouse and up the rise to the Forth Bridge. At half-glass I had to put on the second injector, and knew in my bones the engine wouldn't stand it. With the one injector, in spite of a smokebox full of ashes, I wasn't doing so badly: but two injectors, plus a vacuum big ejector …"Oh well," I thought, "everybody must get a cold run sometime; this is yours."

So I "filled her up" as we rumbled over the Bridge, and tried to get the pressure back with the use of the blower as we coasted down to Inverkeithing. It was hopeless. The smokebox ashes possibly were partly responsible, but the way that vacuum brake was being used had a lot to do with it.

If you have any acquaintance with the vacuum you know that it isn't so quick in effect as the Westinghouse. My mate kept on pulling down the application handle until he did feel an effect, and by that time we were round the curve at fifty instead of twenty-five, and he was trying to blow the brakes off with everything he had. We were now almost at a standstill, in spite of a wide-open throttle and the reverser in full fore gear, and thus we continued up the next bank until I tapped him on the shoulder.

"I'm afraid you'll have to stop at Dunfermline," I said. "The boiler's near empty, and I've only *two* injectors. They've been on since Turnhouse and they can't put in what you are taking out."

If I'd kicked him in the pants he couldn't have reacted more violently. The air was blue, and I was treated to a flow of "Billingsgate" which even in those rough days must have been unique. But he could do no other than stop at the water-column and not only fill the boiler but the tank as well; and this was only half way on a trip which a "Scott" normally did on well under one tank of water.

I'll draw a veil over the remainder of our run to Perth. When I suggested we might save water if the vacuum "wee" ejector was used instead of the big one, all I got in reply was a grunt (he specialised in grunts). So we ploughed our way northwards, and the start of the long descent of Glenfarg has never been so thankfully reached, I'll swear, as it was that morning.

There was a full-blown row after that performance. "The Brute," as I've already said, "went to town" in his condemnation, and once again I was searching my soul about the wisdom of trying to become an engineman. "He may be right," I thought: "why not pack up rather than get the sack?" But strangely enough the man who first tried to force me to "pack up" was the one who refused to believe what "The Brute" said of me.

I waited for the outcome of that "cold run", and the longer I waited the less could I bring myself to leave the job. Gradually it dawned on me that nothing was happening. There was no letter of dismissal. Instead I was rostered with another driver.

I never learned till years later that my "God in the bowler hat," Big Jim Lawrie, the man who tried to make me change my mind about a career on the footplate was now determined to help me to go on. What he said to "The Brute" I never learned, but whatever it was must have been effective, for I understand he was a much-sought-after-mate in later years.

But let's talk of happier things. I've merely uttered this note of discord to show that all my "geese weren't swans." I'm really not concerned with the "geese" in this book. I want to tell of the highlights by a few of the elite and right now would like to introduce you to one of them.

When I first mated Jock Bartholomew somewhere about 1912-13 he wasn't the well-known figure he became between the two world wars. Off-hand, I would say that he was the most widely known Scottish locomotiveman on the London & North Eastern system after the grouping of the old companies. For many years he represented Scotland as a member of the L.N.E.R. Sectional Council, and finished his railway career in 1950 as Chief Motive Power Inspector for the Scottish Region of British Railways.

He is, I believe, the only living representative of that heroic band who fired the Reid Atlantics as they were first built. And to obtain the real picture of what it was like I had a "crack" with him before writing this chapter.

"Did you like them Jock?" I asked.

"Like them!" he exclaimed. "Look Norman, no man could *like* the N.B. Atlantics. I fired them and drove them. I have had them as regular engines on regular trains for years, yet I could never claim to be on as intimate terms with the Reid Atlantics as I was with other types of North British engines. You didn't drive or fire the Atlantics: you *fought* them."

Then Jock told me something of the battles waged between engines and men away back in 1907-8, when the N.B. Atlantics were "saturated steam" engines with two 21 inch outside cylinders capable of devouring steam at such a rate that it took something like eleven tons of coal to generate the power—and this on a return trip of 266 miles with a capacity load of 350 tons, the tonnage carried by the largest N.B. engine on the Aberdeen-Edinburgh stretch.

There was no "front cage" on the Atlantic tender, so the fireman's first job was to fill the sloping firebox with the ton or two of huge lumps of coal which were built up on the tender front to nearly tunnel height. This was a *must,* for once the engine started to run, those two great outside cylinders caused her to roll like a ship in the sea, and it was no joke to have the cab half-filled with coal, which was the inevitable result if you didn't take steps to prevent it.

So the firebox was filled before leaving the shed. But once on the road the blast soon sorted that and the fireman just became a machine for replenishment. This was expected and nobody grumbled; but it was exasperating to fire those engines for over three solid hours to Aberdeen and three hours back, on a footplate which was dancing under your feet like those "cakewalks" you used to see at a fair, and get no satisfactory result. The old "saturated" Atlantics just would not steam.

They were well named "saturated," too, for not only did the steam from the boilers contain a big percentage of water, but the cab also got its share. There was hardly a steampipe joint in the cab which wasn't perpetually blowing. From the cab roof the condensed steam showered like the monsoon, a heavy shower which the pitching, rolling Atlantic scattered in profusion with a grand impartiality, over driver and fireman alike.

This continual leaking of the Atlantic steampipes may have been due to one or maybe two causes. They were possibly, when running at speed, the worst riding engines on the North British. The bangs, crashes, pitching and rolling of them on junctions and when rounding curves were unbelievable. It was commonly said of them they wouldn't overturn, and most of the N.B. engine-men believed this, until one did overturn and landed itself and its train in a field.

No wonder the pipe joints could not stand up to this sort of thing. However, the common practice of keeping the boiler full may also have had something to do with it. And it was important on the Atlantic to keep the boiler full of water. For one thing, the Edinburgh-Aberdeen road is just a series of twisting ups-and-downs. As one American journalist travelling on the footplate said to me: "Geel if you lads aren't going up or down, you're going round corners, but boyl do you run!"

So when the Atlantic tore up a 1 in 70 gradient and threw herself down the next, the water in the boiler was surging all over the place. Not only that, but due to the difficulty of generating steam, the drivers insisted that the water level should be such as left as little room as possible for steam space; "it was easier to fill up," was their theory.

Jock Bartholomew used to swear there was no room at all for steam, which now and again proved more than a little dangerous. There was that incident in Queensferry North tunnel, when one Atlantic "caught the water" during a slip.

She was pounding up the heavy gradient when her wheels went into a violent spin on the greasy rail. The sudden rush of steam from the boiler (which was needed to supply the increased demand from the cylinders) brought with it a stream of water. When this happens, the throttle valve is jammed open with hydraulic power, and "all the kings' horses" won't shut it. The violence of the resulting slip broke the rail under the pounding of the driving wheels. That's the kind of engine the N.B. Atlantic was.

There was another occasion on which this broken rail had a bearing and which Jock himself experienced. A few miles from the scene of that broken rail, Jock, when driving an Atlantic, closed the throttle to coast down a long bank. At least he went through the motions of closing the throttle.

Nothing happened. The throttle handle was in the closed position, but the throttle valve remained full open, and they were roaring down that hill full belt.

There's a technique for broken throttle valve rods which every engineman knows and hopes he has never to put into effect. Jock tried it. He brought the reverser up nearly into centre, and declares he could have controlled the engine with this and the brake, but he remembered that broken rail and very wisely stopped at the foot of the hill for an engine to tie on and so give him ample control up that bank and into Edinburgh.

Jock recalled the fact that the first of the Reid Atlantics was fitted with a steam reverser, which was merely a horizontal steam cylinder coupled to the reversing lever. It would not stay put when notched up, and it was common practice to have an iron plate to insert in a notch of the quadrant to prevent the lever shooting into "full forward" after it was notched up.

Quite often the steam piston for the reverser went on strike. It would neither move back or forward. So the top part of the lever was taken from the box on the tender where it was carried and bolted on, and the engine reversed or notched up by hand. Eventually the useless steam apparatus was scrapped and the N.B. Atlantic finished her days without any mechanical aid, so far as the reverser was concerned.

Neither had they mechanical lubricators as Jock Bartholomew first knew them. There was a wee two-feed "sight" lubricator to oil the valves, but the cylinders had to make do with an occasional dose of oil poured through oil cups on either side of the smokebox. This, of course, could only be done when the engine was standing at a station. At each stop it was the fireman's job to nip to the fore-end with the "tallow-kettle" and pour cylinder oil, or a mixture of this and melted tallow, into the cylinder oil cups.

It was on one occasion when Jock was doing this at Leuchars that he discovered a fine fat partridge lying stunned on the bogie table. Jock grabbed it, and as I listened to him telling the yarn of what happened after and heard the old familiar chuckle, it carried me back to my young days, when to fire to Jock was an unending joy.

The yarn about the partridge really came out as a result of a casual crack I made about the cleaning of the Atlantics at Haymarket, which was in the super class, even in those days of ultra-clean engines. The four Atlantics each had two cleaners attached to them, whose sole duty was to clean the engine and nothing else each twelve-hour shift. They did not even touch the tender, which was dealt with by the cleaning squad.

Part of this cleaning technique, as I have mentioned already, was a final smearing with tallow of all the polished outside steelwork. This tallow acted like a fly-paper as the engines tore through the countryside. At the end of the trip the buffers, and every part of the smokebox was an entomologist's dream, coated half-an-inch thick with every conceivable member of the insect family.

Some queer things landed on the bogie table, too. I have practically stocked a children's school with specimens of owls, bats, and other kindred specimens, picked off various parts of a locomotive at the end of a run. Most of them, of course, were dead, but Jock's partridge was merely stunned and coming to life when he grabbed it.

Partridge in those days wasn't a usual addition to a locomotiveman's diet, and naturally Jock was pleased, but being single and something of a "bighearted Arthur," he magnanimously insisted that his married driver Bob Ellis should take the bird. So it was stuffed into Bob's capacious "tommy-can." (The "piece-boxes" of a driver and fireman on the Aberdeen had to be big to carry the replacements of tissues, blood and sinews which working the Atlantics over twelve hours involved). Unfortunately, neither Jock or Bob took the precaution to wring the bird's neck, or do whatever one does with partridges before they're cooked. So Bob wandered home with an instrument of destruction under his arm.

When the lid of the "tommy-box" was opened that partridge erupted with the speed and rattle of a machine gun bullet. It hit the roof with a force to bring down the plaster. With devilish purpose in the whirring flap of its wings it crashed into every movable object in the room until it literally rained destruction and finalised its mad career by plunging the room in darkness before making for the window, where a puny pane of glass was no barrier to its urge for the wide open spaces.

Bob had a gift of terse expression. "Just try," he said bitterly to Jock next day, *"just try* to whisper the word 'partridge' to me as long as you live, and by the holy bejabers I'll do to you what I should have done to that damned bird last night."

And so we "cracked " in 1957 of the days and engines of the 1900-1914 era, when Haymarket housed not only Reid Atlantics but Drummonds and Holmes 4-4-0s on which we both had something to say.

But we didn't call them "Drummonds," "Reids," "Holmes" or any of other names beloved of the purists. We spoke of the "730" class, or the "Intermediate bogies" or the "595" class with their seven foot drivers, or the tiny "420s" for which I had a special affection, funnily enough founded on the fact that their bogie wheels were as far as I remember the only ones which were solid discs.

Then somehow the N.B. single-wheeler cropped up and that started something. Jock and I did our best to remember whether it was or was not on one of these that we piloted the 4.45pm Edinburgh to Hawick up the bank to Falahill—a distance of some 19 miles.

Jock's description of that run was more picturesque than strictly accurate. "It was just like being on a glorified flipping mangle," was how he put it. And into my mind came the picture of that airy-fairy experience of crashing through the junction at Portobello and trying to fire an engine which apparently had no wheels to her. Neither had she much shelter from the elements in the tiny cab, nor would she steam; nor was she expected to, for up to then her dead strength had been on the "sea-shore express," a local to Dunbar.

But with the utmost *sang-froid* we had the temerity to "assist" this hard-run train. Jock swears the train engine pushed us up the bank, for the feeble exhaust which came from the "single-wheeler" couldn't have blown the hairs off a gooseberry.

We gave her everything we'd got, including the throttle opening and all the coals on the minute tender, which is about all that I can recollect of that trip, except that the engine and tender were so slack-coupled that I was giving a pretty good demonstration of how to do the "splits" as my legs opened and closed to a high degree of "minimum and maximum" while the engine plunged feebly forward, almost leaving the tender behind her.

Miraculously we reached the top of Falahill, managed to slack the coupling, and tottered out of the way into the loop and a much-needed water-column. Our tank was bone-dry, and at first I thought it would have to remain that way for the water-column bag was frozen solid. It needed all Jock's real muscle plus a coal hammer to bend that leather bag.

It never occurred to either of us that we should have been thankful the water wasn't also frozen. That was the kind of day it was, as I stood and surveyed a bleak white vista of snow-buried mountain from the small eminence of an N.B. single-wheeler's tender. That and the run home tender-first is my most vivid recollection of what now must be considered as a first-hand experience of the legendary past. That, I think (and Jock agrees), must also have been one of the last runs seriously attempted on an express train with this class.

Both of us pondered a minute in 1957 as to whether we had made railway history. Both of us came to the conclusion that we didn't know. We couldn't even remember the number of the engine. We even admitted to each other that we weren't greatly interested then in railway history. That, of course, is the way of enginemen. They're concerned with creating an effect; the impressions are left to those who are interested in them.

The effects we occasionally produced prior to 1914 weren't too bad, when it is remembered that the tiny "420" class were regularly running on express passenger trains whose timings compare favourably with those of today. This at a time when it was the job of a small 0-6-0 to haul a slack-coupled freight train a distance of nearly 140 miles, at speeds which could only be done by a superlative knowledge and work with the engine brakes without much else in the way of stopping power.

Jock fired on such a train and it was certainly a tough proposition to "pack 'em in" continuously for nearly a full shift, work the hand-brake, clean the fire half-way on the trip, shovel forward the coal on the tender to bring it within reach, and face a nasty report if you were even minutes out of your schedule in arriving at your far-flung destination.

I hate drooling "out of my beard" and never consciously indulge in it, but I must confess that as I sat chatting to ex-Chief Inspector John Bartholomew and looked at the still, soldierly build of him, at the clear eyes, ruddy complexion, and shock of still gingery hair, my first impression of him still held. They just don't breed his type any more.

When I mated him first he stood for all I was seeking. Something more than merely a driver of railway engines, I was seeking "a modern" with the ability to use his past experience as a foundation on which to build new techniques in a changing future (not that I put it that way prior to 1914). Somehow I sensed change was imminent, and in firing to Jock Bartholomew fate was kind to a boy who would have been considered a "crank" if his thoughts had been known. Jock Bartholomew quite unwittingly verified these thoughts which were only expressed many years later.

Perhaps I should explain further before leaving a locomotive age which is now (perhaps happily) as dead as the dodo.

V

An Era Ends

The year 1914 is quite clearly placed in my mind as the end of a locomotive era which commenced with the *Rocket* at Rainhill, an era through which passed the great 1895 East-West races and the engines and men who were directly concerned with that mad escapade.

It was an era when enginemen were naive to the point of simplicity, a simplicity which sincerely believed that little existed of any real locomotive value outside the boundaries of their own particular company. It was an era when vendettas were as fierce as the blood feuds of Corsica, and the loyalties to engines and mates were beyond understanding.

It was an era where locomotive Superintendents became "Willie Reid," "Matha Holmes" or "Dugald Drummond" (behind their backs) but to meet them in the flesh assumed the importance, the terror, or the celestial joy of a contact with something as imponderable as the Delphic Oracle on Olympus. It was an era of brilliant enginemenship and not so brilliant: when a man like bearded Davy Strachan could say to me, with only hearing as his guide, "Awa' an book the left big end to washer up"; and when I asked him how he knew which was which when he was fifty yards away from the moving engine, his only reply was: "Och, a' ken the sounds of her."

It was the era where one not-so-brilliant driver was known to collect horse dung and have it sucked from a pail up the overflow pipes of the injectors so that it would stop the leaking tubes in the boiler from the inside.

But it was a happy era where laughter wasn't slightly ersatz, because what the mind doesn't know the heart doesn't grieve over. And we didn't know a great deal.

It was the age when the mess-room was a debating place on everything locomotive (I cannot recall even hearing the words "nap" or "pontoon"). The N.B. "bothy," which is the Scottish agricultural name we give our mess-rooms in those less refined days, was a place of glorious discussion—glorious and quite often funny, to those with the mind, the knowledge and the tolerance to enjoy it.

Jock Bartholomew had all these qualities, and because of that became the leader of the Haymarket band as naturally as the white crest to an oncoming wave. He was destined later to lead a few stormy waves. He not only led them, he also controlled their motion—that, however, has no part in this yarn. To me he was that *rara avis, a* mate who could practise efficiency and expound it, a born teacher with a mental horizon as boundless as the sea. Firing engines to Jock made each day something to look forward to.

Jock's "crack" on the mechanics of the job were interspersed with casual pointers from music, art, and classical literature, blended with a humour, the quality of which I was convinced was truly and fully understood by only one out of his many admiring mates, myself. (I must have been a little egoist, had I had the sense to know it). In my mind I elevated the quite unknowing Jock to the position of "pattern to be followed" by the future driver McKillop.

Jock Bartholomew (again quite unwittingly) was the first to indicate to me that driving locomotives could be a happy experience. Up till then I had treated this phobia of mine very seriously, but now to the textbook was added a little something from the free library, to act as jam to the pill of mental endeavour.

The few years I spent on the spare were my most rewarding as a fireman. During those years I made acquaintances of most of the N.B. engines, if not intimately, at least sufficiently well to allow me to say I fired on them all, with one or two never-to-be-forgotten days with an Atlantic.

One of these days nearly made me hand in my resignation, for I realised from that short sixty-mile trip to Dundee and the same distance back that this was about my limit. Not only that, but it let me into another secret. This particular trip proved to me that on the N.B. Atlantic, it wasn't sufficient for the fireman to have good arm, shoulder, and stomach muscles, it was also necessary to have legs made of flexible iron, at least on this particular engine, No. 876.

When I set off I was communing with myself for the first two or three miles "Don't know what makes them look on these regular firemen on the Aberdeen's as supermen. Nothing to it," I mused as I whanged the coals into that firebox. That on the first few miles, before we started to really run.

Through Turnhouse is possibly the fastest stretch on the first sixty miles to Aberdeen and it was here that my communion ceased to be cynical about the "regulars." *Waverley* (that was her name and I'll never forget it) started to roll, not just the solid roll I had experienced on any other type of engine previously, but a bogie-to-trailing-wheel crashing pitch which seemed to me to be doing its best to wrench the engine apart.

I thought something was seriously wrong and as I clung on for dear life, fixed immovable in my seat, I looked at the driver expecting him to be doing an emergency act. He couldn't have looked more unconcerned; he was twiddling a bit of cotton waste, and gave it a wave towards the fire-hole as an indication that I could keep on firing. I wished I hadn't looked at him.

There was nothing else for it, so into the middle of that devilishly heaving cab I ventured, grabbed the shovel, and tried to get coals through the narrow hole in the firebox. I signally failed to do any such thing. I just couldn't stand on the footplate without holding on to something, so for the few hectic minutes this wild burst lasted, I practised "one-hand firing" as was done on every other N.B. type except the Atlantic.

I held on with one hand, jammed the shovel into the coal-hole of the tender, brought the full shovel quickly round and rested it on the mouth of the firebox. Then with my right hand I worked the fire-door handle to open the door, shot the coals as far as I could with my left hand, then quickly shut the door, and repeated the process, until we sailed on to the Forth Bridge at a mild "forty."

This was my chance to open the fire-door and "bang them in" with both hands. But even on the Bridge my toes were trying to find a grip inside my boots, for in place of the high-speed pitching roll, *Waverley* proceeded across the Bridge with a motion not unlike that encountered by a novice the first time he sits on a cantering horse. If you've ever experienced this you'll know it means that the rider generally reverses his up and down motion to that of the horse, and finds himself coming down when the saddle is coming up.

That's what my feet were doing on the Forth Bridge. I was bouncing like a tennis ball on a racket. On no other type of engine can I recall such a buck-jumping exhibition being put on as a reaction to this world-famous structure. The Forth Bridge is, of course, peculiar to itself. For all the sounds and movements set up in a locomotive, an engineman could pick out the Bridge if he was blind, deaf or half dead; but never were they so accentuated as they were on that N.B. Atlantic.

So we swept round the corners, we climbed, and then hurtled downwards, with my legs doing their best to withstand the thousand-and-one bashes and strains to which they were being subjected. When we "loused off" at Dundee I had to look at them to make sure they were still attached to my trunk.

Fortunately we had ninety minutes before returning, and while this was spent trimming the coal on the tender, cleaning the fire and other necessary chores, anything was better than that diabolical jigging, heaving turmoil I had experienced for sixty miles. Privily I sought a lone corner and put to practical use the little I knew of massage, to ease my joints and encourage the blood flow from my extremities to my hips. I was certainly glad to finish that return trip and see Haymarket once more. Strangely enough, I completely forgot to be elated that in spite of my sorrows I had got good steam from the engine the whole road.

My mate was the only one who was satisfied with that trip, and little did he know the reason for my lack of response, when he "cracked" genially; "Good trip, Norman. When are you coming with me again?" My sole desire at that moment was a big warm bath, where I could lie down and die in comfort.

I didn't die then or thereafter, possibly because that was the last time I ever fired an N.B. Atlantic and frankly I am not sorry that fate willed it that way. The 1910-14 years were full enough of toil to satisfy even my urge for the "he-man" heroics, without going to the extreme limit of self-immolation by inviting the *coup de grace* on an engine that no one would love except perhaps her designer, who evidently forgot that while it's easy to make an engine devour coal with the appetite of a glutton and behave like a ship in a storm while doing so, providence wouldn't team up by producing a shock-resistant human being to feed her.

So I was content occasionally to fire the "730" class on the fifty miles or so to Glasgow as a spare fireman, and liked them a lot. They had a wheel reverser which formed the driver's seat, and a bigger number of smaller notches for setting the valve cut-off than the Atlantic reversing lever quadrant. They rode and steamed very well, and were easy to fire—which two latter statements couldn't be made with freedom about the superheated N.B. "Scotts" which, if I remember correctly, were coming into prominence round about 1912-14. In point of fact the Reid superheated 4-4-0s which carried the names made famous in the books written by Sir Walter Scott, created not a little misery among the regular drivers to whom they were allocated.

They rode wonderfully well (for an N.B. engine) but just would not steam. As no excuses were taken then for losing time on main line trains, the drivers and firemen had a pretty thin time of it during these early days, much more so than they would have nowadays. For it was decided by authority without any hope of appeal whether a man was to remain in a certain "link" or not.

This was a serious matter for any driver who had managed to rise to main line working, as the rate of wages was governed by the trains which they worked. For instance the Edinburgh-Glasgow main line drivers were paid 6s. 6d. per day and when one of them was taken off the job because it was alleged he mismanaged the operation of the "Scott" he drove, it meant a drop in earnings of one and sixpence a day.

The controversy which raged in the Haymarket bothy about this "mysterious" type was worth hearing. For in two ways at least they were regarded as difficult to understand. Firstly, there was this "new-fangled" superheat apparatus which obviously took up more than its share of the space which should have been given to generate steam pressure. So said the "bothy orators." Secondly, there was this business of the "rocking shaft." Why on earth does a man build an engine, set the eccentrics on the shaft to work the valves one way, then deliberately, by interposing a "rocking shaft," make the valves move in the opposite direction? This was the "mystery" of superheat and inside and outside admission queried by hundreds of enginemen on the North British Railway, some forty-odd years ago.

Nowadays it is easy to smile at the seeming simplicity of these days (some of us may possibly call it "ignorance"), but it should be remembered that in the pre-first World War era, railway officials weren't tumbling over themselves to enlighten their enginemen on the new advances in design as they are in this age of free and unlimited aids to education. What the enginemen learned, he had to go after in his own time, and spend his own money in obtaining it. Much of his locomotive knowledge he obtained, handed down as a formula from driver to fireman, and of course once the formula did not apply, it took quite a bit of mental adjustment, coupled with a lot of trial and error, before many could accept what to them seemed the overturning of well-tried and accepted practices.

I would like to give just one example of this in illustration. One old driver told me in all seriousness when "tutoring" me on how to test a piston to see if the rings were defective, "of course, Norman, that's the way to do it if she's a saturated steam engine; but if she's wan o' th new-fangled superheaters ye'll hae tae dae it the opposite way for they are 'inside' no' outside' admission engines."

This isn't a text book, and in inflicting this illustration on the non-technically minded, I should perhaps explain that "inside" or "outside" admission steam has nothing whatever to do with the pistons; it alludes to the admission of steam from the boiler to the steam chest, before reaching the pistons, which of course are driven by the steam in exactly the same way, no matter what the "admission" is.

It was left to drivers like Jock Bartholomew and a few others who were "modern" to try and explain the difficulties which arose in those early days of slow advancement in locomotive design. But it was an uphill task without assistance or even encouragement from the "blokes at the top."

One benefit I personally received from the furious discussions which went on about the new engines. For quite a while I had been trying to absorb a course on steam engineering, and as I've said, I was a "lone wolf" in this. I dared not tell a soul that I was seriously endeavouring to understand the language of "my betters." Had I told any of my mates what I was doing they would have thought I was a crank. At least so I thought. Now looking back from the sense which comes with the years, it's just possible that I was too immature to even risk ridicule.

Whatever it was, I was finding it extremely difficult and was convinced I was making little or no progress in putting something "under my hat." One day, however, I listened in to a discourse from one of the acknowledged bothy "genmen," whose word on locomotive "know-how" was accepted as the final dictum on the matter.

He was in full flight on the favourite topic of the times, the "rocking shaft" and was elaborating on "valve gears and their function," when I cocked my ears. What he was saying was palpably wrong and quite unconsciously I said so to myself. Although the thought was unspoken I went all hot and cold, for it must be remembered that in those days it was almost heresy for a youngster to contradict a driver. But I *knew* he was wrong and I was confident I knew. It hit me for the first time that my laborious grind to understand the technicalities was not so futile as I had imagined. I had been on the point of giving up—but not now. I lapped up the text books after that like a cat does cream. To the technical classes I was attending, was added a correspondence course. I hadn't a bean to spend for a year after this.

I shovelled coal with gay nonchalance, for in the firebox I was seeing not just flames. I was "seeing" a barrage of electrons, "unseen" by my mates. Electrons with no weight, something you could feel, that could and did *actually* make their way into the water through the copper of the very firebox I was packing 'em into. I was "seeing" heat.

This wasn't a job, it was fun and games! Every exhaust beat from the engine chimney, every clink from the valve gear, every single thing the engine did, became either a verification of something learned, or a fascinating problem to be taken home or to the good fellow who was suffering me at the technical college. This wasn't a job, it was a way of life! And all this because "Willie" Reid built an engine with a rocking shaft.

Nevertheless, I went on boxing, swimming, and running, for the rule that "children are seen, not heard" was still very much in evidence, as I found one day when, in a moment of spontaneous bonhomie, I broke into a "technical talk" while firing to a grand, old, salted die-hard. His cold look developed into as near a sneer as his benevolent old soul would allow as he reproved me. "Yell hae tae be a driver a long time before ye unnerstaund 'a aboot that, laddie," he observed.

I didn't think it then, but I do know now, that he was dead right. All the technicalities in the world could not make me an engineman: could not, for instance, give me the "feel" which that old lad demonstrated even as he spoke, by closing the throttle, and without apparently looking at the road ahead, push the Westinghouse brake handle forward with certain and meticulous exactitude, to bring us to a gliding stop as if we were on greased velvet.

Could I do that? Would I survive firing the Atlantics ? I wondered.

I needn't have worried. Away in Serbia a bomb exploded and an Archduke died; an Emperor got mad, fighting mad, and in the first flush of excitement a steady way of *life* was thrown into the discard in more places than Haymarket locomotive shed. So let's take a brief look at Haymarket, and at the North British, for although I didn't know it, the blast from that bomb in Sarajevo swept away an era never to return. Had I known this perhaps I might have taken a much closer look at the time than I did.

To take a look at the North British Railway in general and my own depot in particular in 1914 will, I suppose, be a pretty fair blueprint of what the sentimentalists like to call "the good old days."

The boundaries of the N.B.R. stretched south to Berwick and Carlisle, north to Perth and Aberdeen, west to Glasgow and east to Edinburgh, with the latter town as the headquarters of the system, although for locomotivemen the headquarters were in Glasgow (Cowlairs) where the engines were built. That is a rough but not meticulous outline of the set-up in 1914.

Within these boundaries we were absolutely on our home ground, and most of the drivers were so familiar with the trip they ran, that I verily believe they could have named every sleeper on the road. Every main line engineman drove to such a rigid formula that it was common to hear such remarks as: "I *always* shut-off at the wee surfaceman's but on the far side of the bridge at so-and-so." This used to agitate my mind quite a lot as I pondered on the many snags to reducing the working of a railway engine on an express train to a formula. Even in those callow days I realised that wind and weather, along with a hundred-and-one other factors, just wouldn't allow that.

But perhaps I was too literally minded, as I found out when I took the trouble of checking up on the passing-point times. Most of the drivers to whom I fired seemed content to ignore the "in-between timings." All that bothered them was the departure and arrival times, and seldom do I remember any of them being called in question on this way of running. In fact most of them had their own points for looking at their watches, which seldom coincided with the points given in the working timetable.

In 1914 all the regular train-men still had their own engines, and as far as I can remember, the system still held good whereby the driver stayed with his engine in the shed when it stopped for its periodical boiler wash-out once a fortnight. (I may be slightly out here, but if this system wasn't in vogue in 1914, it couldn't have been stopped very long as I have clear recollections of the orgies of gland-packing, gauge glass renewing, and all the fun-and-games of cleaning which went on during those shed days).

Having their own engines on their own runs, year in and year out, the drivers of my young days were so familiar with every detail of road and machine, therefore, that what they did and why, was shrouded in mystery to myself. I couldn't believe my common or garden mentality would ever absorb it all.

To give one instance of this. In 1914 I just couldn't believe I'd ever remember the position of every single signal on the roads we ran. And maybe it is easier to understand my doubts if it is remembered that there were no yellow aspects shown in distant signals on the N.B. in 1914. At night they either showed *red* or green, and we gaily sailed through distant signals showing the "danger" aspect without a care in the world.

There were no "easy trips" as we know them nowadays. The engines were difficult to fire and drive, and both driver and fireman never even expected to feel comfortable while running a train. With the exception of the Atlantic the seats provided for the engine crew hardly deserved the name—they were mostly a few square inches of wood, the top of the reversing wheel on the Holmes "seven-footers" or sometimes nothing at all.

The regulator handle had so little leverage (it was stuck in the centre of the boiler end) that it was common practice for the driver to use his foot to open the second or "big" valve, and when he couldn't do this semi-contortionist act, it was a two-man four-handed-effort by his fireman and himself to get that throttle "over the knot." There were other ways of opening the "big" valve but it would take about a chapter to outline them, so I'll refrain.

I've already mentioned the one-handed-firing method universally practised on the N.B.R.; what I haven't mentioned is the fact that it was done with the *left* hand. This was mainly because the engines weren't free enough steamers to allow the fire door to be opened sufficiently long to "pack in a round," plus the fact that the old N.B. fire door handle was on the right-hand side, and the door itself swung *inside* the firebox to form a deflector plate.

There was also the unwritten law that it wasn't the done thing to turn your back to the driver when firing, and this wasn't just a phoney idea. I heard one driver admonish his mate for attempting to fire right-handed. "None of yer coup-cairt firing here," he commanded, "turn round and fire properly!"

I got the almost heretical idea that it was a racket, this locomotive game as practised in 1914, as the underlying motive appeared to be: "If it's not difficult to do, then it's not being done properly." I was inclined even then to question the primitive, and we were primitive in many ways.

There was not a single power tool in my depot to assist the fitters in their job of servicing the engines. Think what it means to bore out, say, a cylinder cover stud with a hand-drill, or turn a big-end brass on a lathe with a foot treadle as the driving force. That was how primitive was a main passenger working engine shed just over forty years ago, and funnily enough, no one appeared to think it should be otherwise.

So we went on our unthinking way—quite happy to belch out smoke and sparks, with never a complaint from anyone as far as I was aware.

When we wanted to tell the signalman anything, either when running or standing, we had only one means of communication, our engine whistles. The amount of ear-splitting noise which characterised the old railways would get half of us sacked if we dared to persist in it today. There was one particular spot, bang outside two rows of tenement buildings, where engines used to stand and "cock-crow" for twenty-four hours on end. The folk in those buildings must have been sound-proof.

That perhaps typifies the railways in 1914 better than any other illustration I could give, because unlike today a railwayman, despite his poor pay, despite his near-primitive conditions of work, and despite the nuisance he must have been to people not of his kind, was a valuable member of the community, with the personal pride which such an assessment gives.

And it was thus we regarded ourselves, when "Kaiser Bill", Emperor of Germany, plunged Europe into a blood-bath, and involved most of the civilised peoples in the first World War on August 4, 1914. A week or so after that date a government poster came out, showing Lord Kitchener pointing a finger, and his eyes looking at you from whatever angle you stared back; underneath the mammoth head and shoulders it said: "Your King and Country need *You!* Taking it literally, I promptly dashed off to fill the need.

It's just as well that I did "get off the mark" quickly, for a government order forbidding railwaymen to join up was issued the following week, but I'd beaten them to it, and was swallowed up in what Ian Hay has described as *The First Hundred Thousand*— Kitchener's army. I'm afraid there was nothing heroic about the business. In principle it was caused by the same reason for which had I wanted to become a locomotiveman. I wanted to prove myself capable of doing something tough, and strange as it may seem my urge to drive engines fitted me better than I knew for it. For I took with me into the army four years of toughening which encouraged the doctor who passed me to write on the form he filled in "Physical condition—Superior." That night I spent a long time in my tiny bathroom flexing my muscles.

And so I left Haymarket, and a railway era ended for me in August 1914. Everybody told me I would be back by Christmas. The last engine I fired that beautiful summer's day was a little eighteen-inch cylinder 0-6-0 goods. The next time I saw one of her kind was nearly four years later, but I wasn't firing her. It was in Mesopotamia (now Iraq) and later I drove that old 0-6-0, but by that time the war was over, and on the driving splasher it carried the name of *Maude,* the G.O.C. under whom I served. But I'm running a bit ahead of my schedule.

VI

C'est la Guerre

I had quite definite ideas about my role in the army (at least before I entered the recruiting office). I did not intend to wear a kilt, although I believe my clan connections give me the right to wear about seven different tartans; I have the right to do that, but quite unsuitable legs! So I was determined not to display my knobbly knees to a stunned world, and I favoured something in the nature of the "Death's Head Hussars," or the Lancers with their beautiful red trousers with a broad yellow stripe.

So I displayed my torso to the doctor, hopped about in the nude, held up my right hand, took an oath to do my duty to the King, and collected a shilling, after which I stated clearly my military desires. The officer whom I addressed merely glanced at my papers, then scrawled the mystic letters "R.E." along a line. It was only when I was out on the street that I learned from a pal that I was enlisted in the Royal Engineers, and bound for their depot in Chatham.

I went back into that recruiting office like a shot out of a gun. "I didn't join up to become an engineer," I carefully explained to the officer. "That's all right sonny," he replied, "none of them do. But all locomotivemen go automatically to the R.E.'s. It's an order my lad, and you're in the army now."

So for the first time I went outwith the boundary set by the North British Railway. I spent an uproarious week at Chatham with a sergeant straight out of Kipling, whose brogue was a delight, and his instructions as he roared the drill for physical jerks a pure joy, until my turn came to pass a trade test, don a blue tunic, trousers, and a convict-like form of forage cap, which was the Kitchener's blue uniform for the "first hundred thousand." I must have passed my test for I was given 2s. 6d. a day extra.

For the years of the war I drew that half-crown a day without earning one halfpenny of it, for from first to last of them I never stepped on the footplate of a railway engine except to look at it. In the language of my new environment, "I dodged the column" and wangled myself into the signal section of the R.E.'s, when I learned that dispatch riding was a "maybe" and that I'd have riding breeches and spurs, and quite possibly a horse to ride. I passed my tests as a dispatch rider all right, I got my spurs, my riding breeches and puttees, but all the dashing I did was from one shell hole to another, or through miles of trenches, with the South Lancs. and the remnants who retreated from Mons with the 12th Brigade.

It was after the battle of Loos that I got kicked out of France— literally kicked out. Apart from a tiny chip out of my arm by a stray shrapnel fragment, I was having the devil's own luck, when I tried to stop a runaway mule, and woke up in hospital. I never even saw it lift its leg to let me have it between the eyes, and it kicked me so successfully that in twenty-four hours I was in a Northumberland war hospital, and most of my family came to take home the body. Someone had transposed "Kicked by a mule" into "Killed by a mule." There were happy rejoicings that the report had been "grossly exaggerated."

They took a few pieces of bone out of my skull, squared off my nose a bit, and I was on my way. They needed signallers and dispatch riders in darkest Africa. I bribed a sergeant-major to get me on to that draft and he succeeded only too well.

If you've never ridden in an open wagon behind an engine throwing wood sparks, in a temperature which reminded me of my firebox days, don't ever wish for the experience. If to this is added miles-thick clouds of red dust, insects as big as your fist, and no food, you don't enjoy it, even if you are interested in railways. The French wagons marked "8 horses, 40 men" were sheer un- adulterated luxury to the *Gharry a moschi,* which is good Swahili for the military trains in which I travelled during the first World War in East Africa. That "Gharry a moschi" which means literally the "cart of smoke" is perhaps indicative of the honest nature of Swahili nomenclature, but is hardly an enticement to gay adventure by rail. I was beginning to appreciate how wrong I was in thinking my North British Railway was a little behind the times.

General Jan Smuts made short work of the Germans in East Africa, and before we knew it, "British East" and "German East" were all one. Jerry was chased out, and the R.E. signals were asked to do a spot of rehabilitation. In the way they have in the army, I'm not quite clear how I became attached to the Indian Telegraphs, but before I knew where I was I was leading 250 African porters and Indian linesmen out of Dar-es-Salaam. So a North British fireman who drew half-a-crown a day for passing a locomotive engineering test which authorised him to drive a locomotive in the British army, spent quite a part of his time tutoring naked Swahilis, or

Kavirondos, or Kikuyus to bind on wires to insulators, his mind all the time wondering how Jock Bartholomew and others were doing, away in small a corner of the world thousands of miles distant.

At Haymarket they were having a real tough time. There was such a dearth of firemen in 1916 that drivers were firing to drivers as senior as themselves, and it was no joke having to pick up a firing shovel for men who had been driving for anything from ten to fifteen years. Jock told me that on one job he had the unique experience of driving for half of the shift, and firing the engine for the other half.

For the first time in the history of the N.B.R. (or any other railway company for that matter) they became merely a part of an all-Britain system with direction from a central point in London. The enginemen at Thurso on the Highland railway became as important as those in London, Edinburgh, or any other place. The war effort shifted the centres of importance to an extent which in our wildest dreams we never would have believed possible and our trade union representatives weren't slow in recognising this.

Where previously each railway company had made their own conditions of service, hours of work, and rates of pay, it was now a government's "baby to hold" and it was obvious that the old order of things must change. It wasn't logical, for instance, that the top link drivers working the North Eastern engines to Newcastle stabled in Haymarket shed, should be paid a higher daily rate than the N.B. drivers working to Aberdeen and whose engines stood in the next road in the same shed. It wasn't logical, either, that on the Caledonian men should have to work eleven hours as a day, while the N.B. men worked ten, and as it was now a national all-out effort, the duplication of trains, the competition, and all the waste these last two factors meant was shown up clearly when the war effort ran up against the old railway company set-up.

Those were a few of the illogicalities, but as is inevitable the big view didn't take much notice of the smaller niceties. The regular engine tied to the same drivers, the time and money spent on cleaning (even if there were cleaners), these and a few more drastic changes struck dismay into the hearts of the drivers who had been brought up in the beliefs of the railway era which started on its way out in 1914. But worst of all was the feeling of impotence of these same drivers, when they complained to the "gaffer," and found that with the best will in the world he could do nothing. The local official had become nothing but a rubber stamp. The personal element had disappeared. For good or ill the real power to do real things was vested elsewhere. I would like to stress that *good* and *ill*.

So unbelievable things started to happen to the engines. Big ends knocked to an extent which had never been heard of before, glands blew volumes of steam, where a mere puff was previously looked upon as almost sacrilege. Filth, dirt, and general disrepair proved to the theorists' satisfaction that a railway locomotive could carry on under appalling treatment.

So these fellows whom I'd left behind plugged on through the war years in the belief that the excuses given for their difficulties would end sometime. "C'est la guerre", they were told, when the "common user" in locomotive power tore their regular engines from them, and they believed what they were told.

Thinking of Haymarket and trekking through East African swamps, I gave little thought to the essentials, and the first essential in the tropics is health. How many times I had malaria I'll never know. You get that way, especially when you are on your own as I was. Something was bound to crack, and I woke up one morning in a Tanga hospital with someone forcing open my burnt-together lips to pour physic into me. Six of my African boys had carried me from Bagomoya to Tanga for five days in the sun, after I'd conked out, and it wasn't only my lips which were burnt after that unprotected grilling. The M.O. pronounced me a total loss so far as the army was concerned, diagnosed cerebral malaria, and shipped me to Cape Town. I lay in Simonstown hospital convinced that I was on my way back to Haymarket—if I was ever fit enough. I don't know that I was any too pleased about it.

The war wasn't over. I liked putting in a strong finish to any job I tackled and to get "my ticket" like this wasn't as I'd pictured it. I'd get well or bust, and to cut it short I nearly did bust, but eventually got sufficiently well to stare straight into the eyes of the president of a medical tribunal in a convalescent camp in England, and say "I'm perfectly fit, sir."

They shoved three stripes on my arm, told me I was an instructor, gave me 108 boys not unlike what I had been myself three years previously, and in a month I had them licked into sufficient shape to take them with me on my third spell of active service. This time it was to Mesopotamia, and I often wondered if any of those boys knew that the "Sarge" who tried to behave like a mixture of Victor Maclaglan and Beau Geste, was really just a

Haymarket fireman putting on an act. That I was not to see Haymarket for another two years I did not know.

The war was over three months before I left Baghdad on my way to demobilisation, and I was diverted to India. Another three months elapsed before the army decided to get me to Liverpool, and from there to Scotland.

Once more I was a civilian, with an erzatz suit of clothes, a few pounds, and a month's leave. For a week I jingled my spurs in front of a rather bored Edinburgh, then chucked them along with my uniform into the dustbin, donned my civvies and made my way to Haymarket.

VII
Where every Prospect Pleases

When I returned to Haymarket I found that I was no longer a spare fireman. Although I had joined the army without asking permission from my betters, the fact that I had done so before the instruction came out forbidding this, automatically entitled me to my promotional seniority all the time I was away. So in 1919 I was a main line fireman.

"Do you want an easy job to break you in?" John Lamond, the foreman, asked me. "No, I didn't want an easy job." So on the footplate of a "Scot" I went on my first day back, and it was quite obvious my driver was nervous.

He was a decent soul and perhaps he had cause to read me a cautionary lecture. "You see, mate," he said, as kindly as he knew how, "the army is bound to make a man lazy and soft—driving and firing these engines on the Glasgow main line is hard work."

I didn't answer at first; I was thinking. I was thinking of that trip through the Suez to the Persian Gulf on that iron ship *The Francis Joseph*. I was seeing my draft 108, or 109 of them if you include an officer, all of them completely "out for the count" with the effects of the heat. I was looking at myself with the iron decks almost burning the soles off my boots, and I was thinking of that ships' hold like an imitation of Dante's Inferno, where I had single-handed brought up every ounce of kit when we arrived at Basra.

I looked at my driver's big white face and his protruding belly. "Yes," I said.

"I know you'll do your best, Norman."

"Yes," I said.

I looked round the cab of my "Scott." It was all there as I'd left it nearly five years ago, except that the gauges were more dirty, the brass of the water-columns black, the cab grimed. I lifted the floor-boards as I was used to. Underneath it was crammed with dross and coal. I looked into the auxiliary oil boxes for the trailing drivers; the trimmings were black with scum.

It was all here, but different, and somehow smaller. I looked into the firebox; it too looked smaller, not nearly as formidable as I used to believe. I tried the shovel—it appeared to be lighter than I remembered. Something had happened, everything seemed to have shrunk—I didn't at first realise that it was I who had altered, mentally and physically.

I knew I needn't any longer regard my engines as beyond me. I grinned at the "clock face" and I'm sure it grinned back.

And it grinned all the way to Glasgow. Steam? We had barrels of it. I treated that "Scott" like an old pal. I even opened the fire door wide and fired her with both hands.

I experimented with her just to see how she would answer back. I'd never have believed it. I let the fire burn down until it was a mere shimmering few inches of white hot flame. Steam? Who said it was hard getting a "Scott" to steam? I could do this for twenty-four hours and enjoy it. My mate never uttered a word. Nor did he speak to me for the remainder of the few weeks I fired to him. He merely sat and stared at me silently as I yanked the floorboards up, cleaned up the unholy mess, cleaned the cab, scoured the brass, and treated the firing part of the job as an incidental "extra" as not worthy of particular thought or worry.

There was in fact nothing to worry about, and it took me quite a while to realise that the reason for this was that I'd lost my *fear* of the job, or may be it was just that I'd grown older.

So in time I made the acquaintance of my first N.B. "Glen." Split-new was this *Glen Garry,* on a split-new train, the "Fife Coast Express," which ran where its title indicated—round one of the most beautiful stretches of coast in Britain. Built like a "Scott" except for her smaller wheels, the "Glen" was a "brain wave." She did the job she was intended to do with such good grace that to this day many of my colleagues who work the type of trains on which the "Scotts" and the "Glens" are booked, would, if they had their choice, have a "Glen" every time.

They were built more especially for the West Highland stretch between Glasgow, Fort William and Mallaig, so my *Glen Garry* was not in her natural environment. But she suited me and we spent a happy time together, after the first few days of discord, which wasn't between her and me, but with my new mate, who also seemed to be bitten by the fear of the returned "swaddie" in all his dreaded incompetence.

The "Fife Coast Express" was an afternoon job which took us to Anstruther, where we remained for the night and returned the following morning to finish in the early afternoon. To me it looked like a picnic, and I was full of grins and bonhomie, until I turned out and saw "Death and Disaster," as I immediately christened the gloomy individual who was to be my mate on this lovely little engine. He went into his routine almost before I could get my coat off. I paid no attention to him as he orated. I merely whistled softly to myself "The Army of today's all right" and went on with my work. But when there was no sign of it ceasing even in the Waverley station I got a bit fed up.

"Look, mate," I said "why not wait till we're on the road, then you'll know if we're going to get steam or not?"

What I was really experiencing, although I did not realise it at the time, was the reaction from the long years of trial my mates had undergone. It was a general condition due to continual long hours on the footplate, and many of the enginemen carried the hall-mark of the 1914-18 years to the day they retired.

My *Glen Garry* fairly pranced to Anstruther, steamed like a dream, and I loved every beat of her. When we stabled her at Anstruther that first night we were informed there were no lodgings for us, and if the moans of my driver were bad before, they-were a good deal worse now. A major disaster couldn't have hit him worse, I thought. I mildly suggested we could "bunk-up" in a carriage of our train. "We could tie on the heater to warm it up, and buy some food in the shops," I said, "We'd be quite comfortable in the carriage."

If I'd suggested sleeping in the local mortuary he couldn't have looked more askance. He gave me one cold glare, turned on his heel and left me. Where he went, I haven't a clue to this day, but each night at Anstruther he drifted silently away—much to my pleasure. As for me, I thoroughly enjoyed myself with *Glen Garry*. I brewed my tea, ate sandwiches until I almost burst; then leisurely and with care I cleaned the entire engine. Away in the west the sun was laying a broad path of gold on a still sea, God was in his heaven, all was well in the world. It was a fitting prelude to peaceful rest. I luxuriated on my couch, the cushions of a railway carriage, until the brightness of day awoke me to the splendour of the sun on my gleaming *Glen Garry*. I sluiced myself from the injector overflow pipe and made my breakfast on the embers in the firing shovel.

I was all ready to grin at "Death and Disaster", but there was no response from him, and so it went on until a few months later I signed my name with a new designation attached to it—*driver*. That was in 1919 and I was still three years on the right side of thirty. I shook hands with my mate, and to my surprise he said "Good luck,

Norman." My reply left him puzzled. "I'm on my way, mate," I said, "on a path where every prospect pleases and only man is vile." He possibly thought I was quite mad.

The driving examination which the returned soldiers were asked to pass on the N.B.R. after the 1914 war was not severe; at least, I did not think so. After an eyesight test similar to that which I passed as a fireman, I was asked a few questions about the Westinghouse brake, a brief query or two about mechanical defects, and I was through—an appointed driver. Nothing about rules, except to read one or two: no practical test on the footplate of an engine on the head of a train: no medical examination as we know it today. But we got a short heart-to-heart talk from the Chief Locomotive Inspector, which went straight to the point.

"We are not being hard on you lads," he said, "We know you can't be expected to have all the answers 'pat' after being away from the job so long. It's up to yourselves now to obtain these answers during the time you are on the pilots, so that you won't let us down when you come on to the more responsible train work. Good luck to your efforts."

"Well, no one could say fairer than that," I thought. Then all sorts of things were born. If that Inspector had been curt or ungracious I'd have gone into battle, but because he acted decently—well, there was one newly appointed driver who wasn't going to let him down.

The very next day the Haymarket Mutual Improvement Class was brought to birth.

The meeting which decided this consisted of two drivers, Jock Bartholomew and myself. For I actually became a driver the day after I passed my test and was never again rostered as a fireman. That was the way of it at Haymarket in 1919. The eight-hours day had made such a demand for enginemen that those of us who were in my year of seniority were lucky.

So Jock and I set the ball rolling in self-education on this game of operating railway engines, in which both of us were more than interested. We had a chat with John Lamond the foreman, who, all in favour of it, promised assistance.

Haymarket came out in a rash of hand-printed bills in the most weird and wonderful assortment of colours I could lay my hands on, and they must have grated on any of my mates who had the least artistic sense. Those bills informed all and sundry that the first meeting of the

Haymarket Mutual Improvement Class would take place the following Sunday, that John Lamond would "take the chair" and that no less a person than Tom Henderson would lecture on the vacuum brake.

All this we promised, yet we hadn't even a diagram or drawing of the apparatus and no hall in which to sit. Nine-tenths of the men at Haymarket had never even heard of a Mutual Improvement Class. But they turned out *en masse that* Sunday afternoon.

We pinched the forms from the "bothy" and rigged up others with planks of wood resting on anything on which we could lay our hands. The first meeting of the properly constituted Haymarket M.I.C. was held in the open shed amongst the engines stabled there. Those who couldn't get seats just stood around. John Lamond said his piece, and explained the idea behind "Mutual Improvement." Jock Bartholomew was elected Chairman, I became the Secretary, and for the first time in the history of my depot, a rallying point for the "engine daft" was created.

That first lecture was the most curious I have ever witnessed over a long number of years of close contact with such classes in many parts of Britain. As I've said, we had none of the usual adjuncts to a lecture, but what we did have was a real engine. So Tom Henderson stood in the cab and orated to us from there.

The vacuum brake was a subject with which the Haymarket men were not too familiar, as we normally worked with the Westinghouse, but already rumours were current about the grouping of the railway companies. We knew that if this took place the "vacuum" would become universal, so most of my mates were keen to get the "know-how."

From Tom Henderson they learned how "nature abhorred a vacuum" and how this natural law was used to apply the brakes on a train. During this "say-so," Tom got in a crack about the N.B. Atlantic vacuum apparatus, with its exhaust pipe hidden inside the boiler and its application handle so far out of normal reach, that "you couldn't apply the brake and at the same time look out of the side window to see where you were going."

Truth to tell, that lecture was one of the most inspiring to which I've listened, for Tom speaking about his job was to me something worth coming a long way to hear. As the "star" driver at Haymarket he was almost legendary. And he didn't confine himself that day strictly to his subject. He actually took us along with him and explained his ideas on braking a train on the Edinburgh and

Aberdeen run, and I must give him the credit for breeding the idea which I introduced years later in our class, namely, now and again to desert the purely mechanical nature of the lectures, and get an experienced engineman of recognised ability to talk to us on how he worked his engine on the trips he ran.

Meantime we met every fortnight and "went to town" on an engine. We roped in the leading fitter, and dismantled in turn almost every part of that locomotive. We tried out the theory as laid down in that counsel of perfection, the textbook, and now and again found that the theorists weren't just right.

For instance, there was the occasion when we simulated a valve defect which the text books insisted meant dismantling the connecting rod from the piston, and working on "one engine only." We didn't do this latter hefty job and made bets with each other as to what would happen when the throttle was opened.

The theory was, that the engine would only move about half a wheel turn before she was stopped by a gush of steam hitting the piston from the wrong side. This didn't happen on the old engine on which we were experimenting. Maybe the textbook forgot that engines grow old, and because of that don't act up to the counsel of perfection in the way in which they are supposed.

Nowadays Haymarket is one of the depots which is as near the "ideal hundred engine shed" as doesn't matter, and among the amenities which were introduced when nearly £100,000 was spent to make it so, was a lecture room for M.I.C. or ambulance meetings. In 1919 there was nothing like this even contemplated, and anything we desired had to be paid for out of our own pockets. We bought an old carriage body and set it on a vacant site at the shed, after rather grudging permission from authority.

Nowadays authority arranges competitions and they fall over themselves to provide facilities in the way of charts, diagrams, sectional models, and lecturers of the best calibre. The teams which win the Mutual Improvement competitions go on Continental or British tours with all the expenses paid by an appreciative management. On the North British in 1919, when I suggested to authority that some assistance should be given the Haymarket class on the grounds that it would lead to higher efficiency at little cost to the company, I was met by extreme coldness.

So the "engine daft" among us *bought* our carriage. We *bought* sectional models of the Walschaerts and Stephenson valve gears, and when our meeting place was practically wrecked by a runaway horse and cart, we didn't look for any help to replace it. We bought another carriage and right now I would like to pay a tribute to the many firms which showed greater vision than our own masters.

This isn't a "plug" for the apparatus makers, but it should be stated that without exception every one to whom I wrote requesting information, diagrams or drawings, really showed that they realised that the more an engine-man knew about injectors, brakes, or any apparatus which was made for locomotives, the more efficiently would that part be used. It is true to say that without this assistance our class would have "dimmed out." As it was, we received hundreds of pounds worth of the finest "gen" material that skill and money could provide. (One firm loaned us a sectional model of an injector which must have cost £500). I have never yet put our indebtedness on record publicly, and would like now to do so, for I have long felt that in the early days of the M.I.C. endeavour at Haymarket many of my mates did not fully appreciate just what such assistance meant to us all. Even today I feel that this is very true.

The Haymarket M.I.C. became not only the focal point for tuition on all things connected with driving and firing engines, it also evolved into a centre where friendships developed, social amenities were arranged, and something like a normal way of life was injected into our working environment—which normality up till then had been conspicuous by its absence. As the Secretary of the class for fifteen years, I hammered away with a slogan which must have registered. I preached the gospel, that "while one-hundred-per-cent efficiency was not easily attained, possibly never would be attained, there was no harm in trying." In season and out I plugged this, and for my insistence have it now permanently under my nose, engraved on a silver plate on the barometer which hangs in the hall of my house, a gift given me when I handed over the secretaryship to a youngster of whom I could say with Kipling—

"Tho' I've leathered you and flayed you,

By the living God that made you,

You're a better man than I am … "

For as a driver I meant what I said to "Death and Disaster." I was on a path "where every prospect pleases" and the reason for that was partly due to the youngsters who mated me in the cabs of the engines I was destined to drive. Many of them did not confine their companionship to the footplate. They came with me into the M.I.C. classroom where they eventually succeeded me as they have now done on the engines I drove.

Here and there I'd like to mention one or two of them, as well as a few colleagues of my own generation, who many years later were given the title "… the elite of enginemen on the East Coast Route," by a writer who knew them well. What that writer did not know was that the background story of what happened at Haymarket to allow those lads to earn that title, was possibly started and built up from 1919 when two "engine daft" drivers founded the Haymarket Mutual Improvement Class.

So from 1919 our course was set for higher efficiency on the footplate, not the seeming efficiency which came of repetition, and the traditional handing down of doing certain things in a certain way. This inevitably led to trouble, as I have recorded in the case of the superheated "Scott" class. I also knew from past experience that the tendency to scoff at the theory was not all to the good. That the textbook was scoffed at there was ample evidence to prove.

One such instance from my personal experience can illustrate this point. It happened on a passenger shunting pilot at a station in Scotland, the name of which couldn't be dragged out of me by wild horses. The driver was of my own generation who believed everything he had been told—literally. He shut down the whole station for a considerable time one day because of a brake defect which he presumed he had cured.

I happened along during the frantic efforts which were being made to try and prise the blocks from the wheels, and pulled a plug of wood from the exhaust port of the Westinghouse triple valve which the driver had carefully shaped and hammered in, because, as he said, "I thought it was an air leak and so-and-so told me an air leak on the Westinghouse should always be prevented."

For the non-technically minded it should be explained that what this lad had done was to allow his brake to be applied, but when he wanted it to release he had plugged up the means for air to escape which would have allowed this. So there his engine stood blocking the place, because someone had told him only part of the story. The M.I.C. men at Haymarket were out to get the full story, and only by practical experiment to reject or confirm what the theorist said. During the years ahead we certainly did a lot of both.

So I went on to the engine which had nearly killed me as a fireman, the Haymarket pilot. My turns with "Andra" Manzie stood me in good stead, and I added a few fancy touches to the technique of goods shunting just to boost my new found ego. This apart, however, I never found myself enamoured of the shunting jobs. I wanted to drive trains, and this became an even greater urge when I went on to the Waverley and found out I was neither a mental telepathist nor psychic, for one needed to be something of both to shunt the way they wanted me to do some thirty-six years ago on the Waverley West End pilot.

There was such an assumption of being happy while living dangerously, that most of the shunters were cultivating the not yet fashionable coronary thrombosis, seemingly quite oblivious to the fact that the prevention lay in their own hands, if they would stop acting like asses—which I wasn't long in telling them. It was the practice at that time to shunt with an almost total disregard of the fixed signals, and again this was due to the traditional "rule-of-thumb" approach to our job, which made a certain type of railwayman think that he had all the answers.

When on my first day a shunter stood at the far end of anything up to twenty carriages, and signalled me to carry on, I looked at the fixed signal. It was "on," so I whistled to let the signalman know we were ready for the road, and waited. Nothing happened—or rather, nothing happened so far as the signal was concerned. Instead, I found a fuming shunter at the engine, wanting to know why the "blankety-blank" I was standing there when he had signalled me away. I pointed to the fixed signal, still showing red.

He was stunned. Didn't I know that it was impossible to work in that way; didn't I know that there was an understanding between the signalman and himself on this shift that it was O.K. to pass the signals? It was all right, he would see that nothing went wrong. He would accept all responsibility—and so on *ad nauseam,* with a hint here and there about the "efficiency" of the "old hands" and an insulting reference to incompetent upstarts.

I let it all "blow off" then said quite calmly; "No signal, no shunt." The vendetta was on. I can honestly say that at no time in my whole driving career have I felt so mentally or physically exhausted as I did during the first few months I spent shunting in that station. The shunters took my attitude as a personal reflection on themselves, while the signalmen simply hated me. I stuck to my guns, but I was caught inevitably.

A signal I couldn't see and a pair of "trap points" open, both of them two carriages behind me, did the trick, and the second carriage was derailed when I went forward as was usual for this particular shunt. Never mind the details of that move, but it gave me the chance to do something I'd long wanted to do.

To the Inspector who made the usual enquiry, I must have seemed queer, for without a word of excuse I said "Driver to blame, Sandy, put it fairly and squarely on yours truly". "Sandy" had no alternative, and that was exactly what I wanted. I was informed that a "caution" was to be placed on my service record as punishment for my negligence. Had I anything to say?

Had I anything to say? Authority just didn't know what it was asking for. I gave a complete and detailed survey of the whole dangerous business and demanded an investigation to clear up the laziness which allowed it.

It was unheard of, such a demand from a young driver. But I insisted, and so far as I was concerned I had no further trouble in doing my job safely and with peace of mind. That I was right was proved shortly after, when another young driver, who "played", rammed his pug into the broadside of a lift of carriages, put two women cleaners in hospital, injured himself, and was "told off" at the resulting inquiry for passing a fixed signal at danger.

That yarn possibly illustrates the guiding rule to which I have worked during the whole of my driving career. It's better to be safe than sorry. This has never meant a fatuous adherence to regimentality for its own sake, for I'm convinced from long experience that efficiency goes hand in hand with lots of things, and one of them on the footplate is greater safety. This I proved to these lads at the Waverley before I parted from them.

Once they came to realise I just would not move without every fixed signal being pulled off, they started to play my way, and my way was to show 'em just how smart was No. 826, the tanky I drove. The technique was all-in, and by that I mean everything to do with shunting passenger stock.

I got my brake to such a state of real usefulness that a mere whiff of air was sufficient to kill the light engine movement like that fabled lad with the steam hammer. I could bring 826 up against a lift of carriages in a gliding diminuendo that finished with the buffers touching gently as a zephyr. There was not a fraction of a second between the shunter connecting the brake pipes and my thrusting the Westinghouse application handle into "full release". At the moment when that came we were off like a shot, the "big valve" wide open in response to the reassuring confidence which a series of dropping semaphore and disc signals gave me of a clear and safe road into the maze of crossings ahead.

Much of the shunting at Waverley consists of untying and retying connections going south, north, and west. There is the bare margin of time to do this, and I think I proved to the shunters who worked with me, that although I'd been a pain in the neck to them when first we met, my way was best. In point of fact I know I did, for when we parted, the lad who first "shot" at me for not doing as he wanted grinned like a Cheshire cat, as he quoted the old Scots farewell song "Will ye no come back again?".

Incidentally a reaction from my own firing days occurred while I was on 826, much to my fireman's surprise. This type of 0-6-0 tank engine, which is still shunting in the Waverley, has a very hot cab in the summer. It was the custom (and occasionally still is) for the driver and fireman to clean not only the outside, but to make a really good job of the brasswork and cab paintwork.

I saw to it that my fireman didn't overdo the very exhausting work in the cab to an extent which nearly ended my career on No. 39. The lad was just as anxious as I was, and possibly a good deal more able to stand up to it than I was at his age, but I wasn't taking any chances, and so organised the cleaning in the cab that he did no more than a bare hour at a time.

There was another curious feature about the Waverley pilots which is worth remarking on, in that while the rest of the enginemen on the North British were working a twelve-or ten-hour day, the work on these pilots was considered so exacting that the crews only worked eight hours a day. Today it is still an "eight hour pilot." Maybe, however, the work isn't quite so exacting as it was when I was expected to dash out and in without positive signal information to keep my mind easy.

When I hear the sentimentalists regretting the advent of the grouping and then the nationalisation of railways, I'm apt to mumble into my beard, for no matter what criticisms can be levelled at remote control there is one of which it can never be accused. It has never to my knowledge penalised or even thought of penalising a driver for insisting on safe working. I should know, for I've tested it out on several occasions.

Today the Waverley station is about the safest place in the world in which to shunt. There's hardly a pair of points which are not signal protected, and electrically safeguarded, while in many other ways the shunting drivers' conditions of work are a great improvement on what they were when I first knew it in 1920-21. One of these conditions made my departure from the Waverley a little difficult and could form the beginning of a fresh chapter in this "march of progress." Progress it was, too, for in 1921 an Act of Parliament was passed which authorised the forming of four group railways and the North British was destined to lose its identity within the London & North Eastern. It was two years later when we at Haymarket felt the repercussion, but in 1921 I felt we were on the way to a wider life, and I didn't want to be left out of it. But again I had to assert myself to satisfy even this laudable desire.

VIII
A New Conception

When my turn came for promotion from the Waverley pilot on to the short trip goods, someone at Haymarket had a brainwave. "Let's save four pounds," said this economist, "by keeping the Waverley pilot drivers where they are, and promote their juniors on to the short trip goods."

The four pounds mentioned was the "transfer money", two pounds paid to myself and two to the driver who took my place at Waverley, which is classified as a sub-depot. By this payment an engineman is posted to the sub-depot and thus saves the travelling time if he had to book on at Haymarket at the beginning and the end of every shift. I nearly turned somersaults when this hit me, and could hardly sleep until I walked into the sanctum of the Haymarket Locomotive Foreman next morning.

I won't go into all the details of that interview, but I stated in the clearest of terms that I wouldn't be found dead on a pilot if there was a train running which I was entitled to drive. John Lamond, the Foreman tried his best to persuade me that a long spell on the Waverley pilot would be to my financial benefit, with two Sundays working out of three, and so on. It was no good. I insisted, and a week later became the proud "part owner" of the engine on which I had fired to Jock Harding.

It wasn't much of a train, this Queensferry Goods, but it suited me for the purpose I had in mind. I wanted to put one or two pet ideas to the test, and these few miles of branch line were ideal for the purpose.

One of my ideas was about the braking of slack-coupled goods trains, and on the "Ferry Goods" I knew I could experiment to my hearts' content without fear of braking couplings or drawbars. Moreover, I knew the regular guards, and believed they were as daft as I was on this railway game.

So I played quietly in the orthodox way for a week or two until I got thoroughly grounded again in all the little local traits which all such trains have. Then one day as Jimmy Bannerman, my fireman, and myself were eating our sandwiches while waiting for traffic, I spoke.

"My child (Jimmy was about fourteen stone), doesn't it strike you we act very like the Grand Old Duke of York as we cavort up and down the wee hills on this train?" I asked. "We march them up the hill and then you spring to that hand brake, twist it on a few turns while we march 'em down again, and so on to infinity if need be. All the time you are performing, I am sitting here with this little handle idle (I patted the steam brake handle), while you're giving a very fair imitation of a tee-totem. This handle can actuate the tender brake just as well as you can, and with a great deal more power than even your massive shoulders can exert."

"I suggest an experiment. Tomorrow you will not touch that tender brake. I shall use my judgment and the inspired skill of mine which must have an outlet."

Next day we did that trip with me working the steam brake in graduations as fine as my sense of feel indicated as we topped each rise and brought the buffers together as we slid down into the next hollow. According to my calculations the reactions on the train were lovely. Before the day was done, we were flying down those dips with all the buffers close, and the couplings slack; then gradually the weight was gathered until all the couplings were tight, and with throttle and brake working in harmony we made a slick job—at least I thought so. Our guard never said a word, good or bad.

Next day Jim had a go at the new technique. He knew the road perfectly as he had been firing on it before I came on the job. So he negotiated the ups and downs as he thought it should be done. I damned him with faint praise. He just grinned and hollered out to the guard: "Did you get a jerk coming over the 'knots' today, Bob?"

"No, but you darned near pulled the drawbar out yesterday. What are you two playing at?" shouted Bob Charters.

Jim's grin was pure joy, and he never lost the opportunity of telling that yarn every time he wanted to put me in my place.

There was no "big and little brother" act between my mate and myself. I was interested in producing an effect, not in creating an impression, and from the word "go" I wanted my fireman in on this game with the same interest in producing the effect as I had myself. Not to the extent of driving the engine (that was all right on the likes of the "Ferry Goods"), but to criticise, suggest, and demonstrate occasionally, when this could be done sensibly. The cult of the omnipotent driver may have been all right in the days of my youth, I am only too ready to admit that, but for myself I was only too well aware that I'd lost a big slice out of the years when I should have been gaining practical experience, and I was out to make that good, my way.

My way was to bring everyone into the picture, discuss every phase of the working, and see how it could be improved. So Bob Charters, our guard on the "Ferry", was told, and we started in earnest to see what was in my ideas. Bob gave me the fastest times he had recorded in his book for years back, and it was now up to me to see if I could do better. But it was to be no "hash and bash" business.

From the minute Bob waved us away, he logged every single item of bad work. If his van was "snatched at" in the most minute degree at starting, if an outsize bump was felt by him as the result of a brake application, or I had his van swaying even momentarily from too high a speed, Bob told me exactly where it happened. It developed into a fascinating game, and did not stop at driving. I was invited to reciprocate about Bob's work. His signals, his shunting technique, or any of the local and peculiar aspects of this particular train. Jimmy, too, got bitten by the game and before long we were almost mind-readers in the way we acted as a team.

It was a crime to "blow-off." Jimmy actually got to a stage in his firing where he could tell the number of times he would use the injector by the size of the train to which we coupled when starting off. He got to such a stage of finesse in graduations of the injector water regulator and the dampers that the amount of coal we had on the tender when we finished the shift made one of my colleagues inquire if it was a "standing pilot" we worked.

Bob Charters was the finest goods guard I have ever encountered. His economy of movement was really superb. He would wander casually along his train, and by the time he reached the van a complete plan was evolved as to how we would dispose of its various sections at the places of call. When we arrived at the yards it was a joy to see him slide the long shunting pole over a buffer, pull it back, and the heavy coupling was off the hook, no matter how quickly we were propelling the lift.

In fact, so slick was this shunting, that I have seen as many as nine "cuts" made, without reversing the engine once, and this was done with little more than a wagon-length of space to work on between the "cuts."

I have expanded on this particular theme for three reasons. Firstly, because I believe that a driver never really gets to know the roads unless he has driven slack-coupled goods trains over them.

(For five years after coming from the Waverley I was fortunate to have the chance of driving all manner of freight and mineral trains over many of the roads served by the North British). Secondly, I have written so much about high-speed passenger train working that it might be forgotten that no driver can do that without going through the mill on what is very often called the less important work. Thirdly, the experimental urge to which I have alluded on the "Ferry Goods" has been with me during the whole of my driving career, and what's more it has served me well on passenger as well as goods train working.

Meantime the grouping had taken place. We were a part of the L.N.E.R. and were now seeing the practical outcome of this change even in our personal appearance. For the first time in history enginemen from London to the far north of Scotland were issued with similar uniforms to wear on duty.

We were rather shy about it all—and no wonder. The first lot of dungarees which came to Haymarket were not exactly "made to measure," although a tape had been run over us by one of the clerks to get some idea of our dimensions. I don't know how it was decided what a man's height was, but I rather suspect they took his girth as a guide, for these dungarees did make the short and fat among us rather like penguins, once we had the legs cut to size, leaving the seats of our pants somewhere in the region of our knees.

On the other hand the skinny ones could almost turn round inside the new uniforms without anyone noticing. Possibly Jock Bartholomew had myself in mind when he penned these particular verses in a long ribald poem on the first issue of uniforms to enginemen.

"With the body of Bacchus and the head of Jove,
I could fill your suit and hat
With an angle here, and a contour there
From folds of rolling fat.
But as I'm small, no size at all
It's pitiful to see
Me try to find my small behind Mids't folds of dungaree."

Dungarees apart, however, we of the North British were learning that there were other engines, and other ways in the railway world, and this was driven home one day when I was given a North Eastern 0-6-0 to work a local goods train. To me that wee engine, more than anything else, pointed the way the enginemen in every part of Britain were destined to go in the future. The water-tight compartment in which we had all been living was wide open.

Two of these wee N.E. goods engines came to Haymarket, one of which was superheated. No. 1858 was the number of the latter, as far as I remember. I never cared for her. The tubes were always leaking, she wouldn't steam, and in many ways was found wanting: Both were classified to take the same loads as their North British counterparts, but neither 1858 or her sister were as strong as, say, *Maude,* of whom more later.

These N.E.'s were, in almost everything, distinct and different from the N.B. engines, and at least one of these differences I didn't much care for, all the driving controls were on the right hand side. To Haymarket men this was like losing an *eye,* or an arm, and we just could not think why a designer should put the driver in the most awkward position he possibly could, and expect him to do his job properly. That was the major moan when N.B. men first drove the N.E. engines.

When I first saw that goods engine, apart from the right hand drive, I was prepared to like her, especially the cab fittings. The seating for both driver and fireman was sensible, while for the first time I experienced the built-up footstools which allowed one to sit on the long box seat with one's legs comfortably rested. On her N.B. counterpart the seat was a few square inches of hinged wood to which even my meagre proportions found it difficult to adhere when running.

The outstanding difference, however, between the two engines was their steam brakes. I'll always remember how startled I was when I made my first application with the N.E. brake. Fortunately, there was no train behind us as I moved the brake handle to a position which, on an N.B. engine, would merely have brought the blocks gently on to the wheels, and slowed the light engine ever so slightly. That N.E. just stopped in her tracks as suddenly as if shot.

For a moment I thought we had come up against some impedimenta (it was dark at the time) and I opened the throttle gingerly after releasing the brake. We sailed on safely, so I decided to get used to that brake before I did any of my fancy braking with the slack-coupled goods train I was going to work. For it is a fact that I had developed a technique with the power brake on goods trains which was proving so successful in practice that I was knocking spots off the timing on every goods train I worked.

Normally, I could run those trains from start to finish without the use of the hand brake, but this meant knowing your brake. So with the N.E., I played safe, and the hand brake was used more on that run than it had been used for months.

There is no doubt about it, the N.E. brake gear was superior to the N.B. type. On the latter, the blocks were much bigger as also were the steam pipes to the brake cylinders, yet I would say the action of the N.E. was at least 25 per cent. more positive, and effective.

I did not care for the "clump-clump" which accompanied me that night. On investigation I found it came from the big flat motion blocks which carried the little ends of the connecting rods. Those blocks walloped up and down on the motion bar, with a degree of play that explained why the piston glands were blowing so badly. We got on all right on that initial run on a very tricky bit of railway, with a more than usually obstreperous type of train: you know the kind I mean. A few empty wagons, then a bunch of coal, followed by quick-moving oil-lubricated vans, then some huge iron girders, and so on. On this road of many ups and downs my train was running on as many as three gradients at the one time, and I particularly liked the way my N.E. engine got her back up against the train when I used her deadly brake, and kept control even if she looked only half as heavy as the engines I was used to on this stretch.

For in almost every respect the N.E. 0-6-0 was more slenderly built. The N.B. wheels were more heavily cast, and carried slabs of balance weights to off-set the heavy marine-type big ends. On those N.E. goods engines there were no balance weights at all as far as I can remember, while the connecting rods and big ends weren't nearly so heavy looking as on my own engines.

Strangely enough, too, I remember remarking to my mate that the lack of weight did not make the N.E. 0-6-0 slip as I'd prophesied on looking her over. If anything, she was surer on her feet than *Maude,* and *she* was about the best of the N.B. 0-6-0s I had handled on this stretch of railway, where there were practically no level sections at all, and where every potential to encourage slipping existed on the twists, turns and gradients of up to 1 in 70.

I had good reason to appreciate what N.B. 0-6-0 *Maude* could do, for I believe I put up what was considered a record run with her on that particular stretch. We had a solid train of coal behind us, and for once got every distant signal. It was shipment coal for South Leith, and we were standing in the docks in twenty minutes dead, from Gorgie

Junction. I have given the times and the names of the places, just in case there is a swifter run to the credit of some other N.B. engine. But I give the credit for that performance to an exceptionally strong engine and the technique I had developed with the steam brake, for thus, early in my driving career, I had come to realise that the brake played a more important part in time-saving than was generally accepted up till then.

Incidentally, the trains I was working about this time were all "to control orders"—another innovation which came with the grouping, if my memory isn't playing me false. Previously it was no unknown thing for goods trains to stand one behind the other in loops and refuge sidings for hours on end. When we were working ten or twelve hours this did not matter so much, but with every engineman claiming payment for every minute over eight hours, some form of supervision was necessary, quite apart from the narrow field surveyed by the signalman on the spot. So a "freight train control" was instituted, and this gave me an opportunity of working a much bigger variety of goods trains and engines than I otherwise would, if I'd been tied to those worked from Haymarket.

I relieved trains and engines from almost every depot in Scotland, and in the process learned more roads than was normal. I was out for every manner of experience I could cram under my hat, and as usual teamed up with everyone with whom I was working. In this case it was the controllers, whom as individuals I never met until years later, but with whose voices I was very familiar on the telephone.

If I finished a run, took the engine to the nearest depot, and there were no more trains to relieve, instead of having an idle hour or two on my hands I would learn another little stretch of local railway, much to my benefit in the years ahead.

On those trains I handled the first "S" (L.N.E. "J37") class 0-6-0 which came out, on a stretch of road which few men at Haymarket ran, and learned her tricks so intimately that later, when driving one regularly, I once undertook to run a goods train from near Edinburgh to Ladder outside of Glasgow without touching the brake from start to finish—a distance of over forty miles.

The 'S' when shut off had a terrific retardation due to compression in the cylinders. The main line between Edinburgh and Glasgow is generally described as level, although like most railroads so described, it is full of subtle little gradients of which only the freight train enginemen are fully aware.

On one occasion my mate and I had an argument about running this road to time. I alleged that, making full use of the road, the brake, and the engine potential, a good slice of time could be clipped off the running. "In fact," I concluded, "I'm willing to bet that on the present timing and with this engine, I could work the train without touching the brake at all—and that does not exclude the possibility of being stopped at signals."

Off we set—(there was one shilling at stake). My fireman was watching the passing point timings like a cat, (the bet laid down that there was to be strict adherence to the timetable) and just to test out my "S" I shut the throttle on the first down gradient to get the feel of the retardation. After that it was "no bother at all." The throttle was eased or opened in degrees to suit the signal sighting distances, the gradients, and the speed we were running as we approached each distant signal, and although we had three of them against us, the retardation of that "S" was sufficient to brake the train. Not even when coming to a final stop in the yard loop was the brake used.

I won my bet, but was parted from the shilling again at the end of that week, when my mate completed the week without the "S" blowing off or showing a wisp of black smoke, yet at the same time keeping the needle of the pressure gauge on the red mark throughout the trip.

That was the sort of thing which really taught me (and incidentally my firemen) something about the ways of the engines we handled. It was all tight to have the answers to the mechanics; it was fit and proper that we shouldn't be a "band of hope" without resource if a defect developed; but our job was to run trains, and only by experience with the throttle in one's hand can that be thoroughly obtained.

By the time I was promoted to the "junior spare" I was ready to take on any type of engine or train Haymarket worked, and by this time the old N.B. horizon had vanished. The invisible barrier at Berwick was down, but I wasn't permitted to penetrate beyond the old confines yet awhile.

It was necessary that, with trains like the "Flying Scotsman," the "Night Scotsman" and the "Aberdonian" now incorporated in the regular train roster worked by Haymarket men, spare men as well as regular train men should know the road between Edinburgh and Newcastle. So a senior spare link was created, of drivers who could step in for the East Coast express men if necessary, or run specials when required. Before I could get on to this link (and did I want that 1) I had to serve my time on the junior spare, which by and large was utilised on trains running on the old N.B. section.

So I started to do a spot of mild passenger work, which wasn't without its benefits. Mostly it was confined to short trips on the type of engines to which I'd been accustomed all my railway days. I learned a lot about saturated steam engines in those days. I also learned a lot about "the rule of thumb" running in which many drivers believed.

I learned, for instance, that a "saturated" engine could go a long distance without lubrication in the fore-end, and that was on a non-stop run of nearly fifty miles. The engine was a Holmes 4-4-0, No. 595, and the trip was between Edinburgh and Glasgow. It was one of those "hurry-up" specials which constantly crop up at Haymarket, where they provide most of the connections for the London trains at Waverley. The engine had been prepared for me, and it was only when I was on the road that I found the *wee* two feed lubricator was passing nothing through the sight-feed.

If that had happened on a superheater we wouldn't have gone two miles before the groans coming from the pistons and valves would have terrified the most stout hearted—to say nothing of the tearing damage it would have caused. As it was, 595 couldn't have cared less. Her seven feet driving wheels flicked the road behind us, there was "nary a cheep" from the fore-end, and neither sight or indication of wear on pistons, valves, or rods. The steam she was generating was saturated all right—so wet that it must have had qualities as effective as the precious oil we pour into them nowadays.

I drove many of the Holmes engines in those days, but developed a real affection for 595. I worked her so often on the double-headed trains so frequently seen on the Edinburgh-Aberdeen road. Most of the regular trains (especially in the summer) were too heavy for the Atlantics and 595 and I was frequently tied on to assist as far as Dundee.

It was about his time that I realised that to quite a few of the regular drivers, the working timetable was merely regarded as an approximate guide. The passing point times were admittedly a bit "haywire" and if they had been religiously adhered to it would have meant that train running was a series of staccato jerks.

To me the timetable was the law, and if it wasn't sensible, then there were proper methods of getting it put right. I believe that from this realisation came my first urge to break down every trip I made into times for running between every signalbox on the road.

As the basis of this I took the time allowed in the working timetable and experimented in running until, when I graduated into the senior spare, I could run an express train on the roads I knew, and under normal circumstances pass every signalbox on the road with no greater fluctuation than fifteen seconds— mostly to the good.

The senior spare meant the London-Edinburgh express trains to me. If anyone had told me away back in 1910 that one day I would have the opportunity of driving the "Flying Scotsman" I would have put it down, as Steinbeck has it, to pure "hooptedoodle." All my engine-daft soul had craved was to drive those bronze-green N.B. Atlantics at the dizzy speed of 60mph Yet here I was with the prospect of the Gresley Pacifics, the N.E. Atlantics, and London stretching away ahead. What better could any engineman ask?

Before this was attained, however, there was a road to learn. I knew the road as far as Berwick, but beyond that lay over sixty-four miles of track to Newcastle of which I knew nothing as a driver or fireman. So for four weeks I lodged at Newcastle and shuttle-cocked back and forward with the N.E. express men.

Up to the time of the grouping the learning of a road was a comparatively easy matter, as a driver had at least some previous experience to fall back on, but with the grouping many drivers found themselves in strange country where they had to literally start from the ground up.

When I returned from the Army I used rather to look down my nose at the fellows who took the trouble to note all the answers down in a book when road-learning, but I saw the sense of it when I started in on that near sixty-five miles of "foreign "railway. For one thing, learning a road on the footplate isn't like driving a car on the Queen's highway. A railway driver has got to *know* every inch of the way. There is no gauge as to where a signal can be looked for. Each section has to be learned off by heart, each signal, bridge, platform, and every little crinkle in the road, every bend, restriction and gradient has got to be printed on his memory, so that daylight or dark, rain, shine, fog, or snow, he knows to a foot exactly where he is.

If there was some form of standardisation or general principle to act as a foundational guide, it would be simple, but there isn't. The only thing that is repeated and has any similarity, is the colour of the signal aspects. Apart from these every section has its own individual peculiarities. And I was too well aware of the fact that there's no margin for error in this game, no allowance for taking chances.

I split that sixty-five miles between Berwick and Newcastle into four parts and drew a complete route map in colour of each section in a book. On one side I showed the up road, on the other the down road, giving a page to each section controlled by a signalbox. If I'd had my way I think I would have inserted each blade of grass by the lineside, so anxious was I to make a go of this opportunity to spread my wings.

It was the late autumn, almost winter, but the gods were kind, the weather was good, and I finished my route map with a pretty exhaustive map lay-out of Newcastle station and the roads right round to Gateshead, over the King Edward bridge, and back over the High Level bridge to the station. The making of this map cost me two sixpences for admission and two afternoons of time, sitting on the top of the old castle looking down on the maze of rails which is the entrance to Newcastle station from the north. From the footplate you get no real idea of how that network of lines flow. But sitting on that tower it became as clear as daylight, and I consider that shilling was well spent.

Of course I didn't need to go to such extraordinary lengths to learn this road, I could have managed with just getting the signals, the landmarks, stations and so on, all taped off, but I was bent on driving my first train on this road with the feeling that I'd known it all my life. It may be a strange thing to say, but I felt I must make friends with this stranger—and before I signed my name in the route book, as now knowing the road between Berwick and Newcastle, I did know it; and somehow I had the feeling that it knew me.

There were others at this same game of learning the road. Quite a few of my buddies were on the spare, and we foregathered at times to discuss the ways and means of driving these new trains. That was many years ago. The road to Newcastle was merely the beginning. Through time Haymarket men were running on to York, and staying in London, but my buddies and I never lost the habit we developed in those early years on the spare. We still discussed how we ran the trains, when as main line express men we "owned" our own Gresleys and drove them day by day on the trains whose names are familiar wherever railways are discussed.

Right now I'd like to introduce you to a few of these colleagues of mine, and before continuing the personal angle in this yarn, recount briefly what they and their engines did.

IX

Big Bill Stevenson

As tough as teak, six feet in length, with breadth in proportion, Bill Stevenson is possibly as well known as any Haymarket driver who ran the London-Edinburgh expresses in the top link. From the very start of his footplate career, Bill was just right for the job. As an earnest of this, Jim Lawrie, "gaffer" at Haymarket when Bill joined the grade in 1908, passed him out as a fireman right away, and sent him back to the village from whence he came to look after a wee tank engine which in those days ran a passenger service between Edinburgh and Dalmeny, the station which gives entrance to the south end of the Forth Bridge. No. 98, a 4-4-0, was stabled at Dalmeny.

As Bill came from Dalmeny it wasn't a hardship (as it was to me) to be asked to lodge away from Haymarket. So Bill scoured and cleaned old 98, enjoying himself hugely through the night and being paid money for what he would have gladly done for nothing. To be in full charge of an engine was payment enough.

It was necessary that anyone left in charge of an engine should be registered as a fireman, so it can be said that Bill Stevenson is one of the few enginemen who served "no apprenticeship" before he passed as a fireman. That is, he served no official apprenticeship. Actually, like myself, he was engine daft, and before coining to Haymarket spent two years working in Dalmeny goods yard as greaser to the examiner who inspected every goods train before it crossed the Bridge.

That was the nearest he could get at his age to being on the footplate. You can bet that like myself he knew a good lot about that "tanky", so he was a success from the very beginning and promotion came his way in due course—promotion, and one or two out-of-the-way experiences.

Being the tough lad he was, Bill was in great demand as a fireman when he was on the spare, and he treated those N.B. Atlantics, which I hated, as his bosom pals. It was all one to him what he was firing; the harder it was, the better he liked it. And it was on an Atlantic that he ran into one of those tragedies on which is built the safety code of the railways of today.

It was in 1911. Bill was firing on the Aberdeen-London fish, the same train as runs into London every morning to this day. These fish trains are hard on a fireman. They are run on little less than an express passenger timing, and are just about twice as solid as a passenger train to haul over the road.

On all the road between Aberdeen and London there is no more difficult stretch than the 133 miles between Aberdeen and Edinburgh. The gradients, the curves and the lashing winds encountered on the north-east coast of Scotland are bad enough on a long passenger train, but on those vans of fish, each of them (in 1911) with four wheels to create extra friction on the rails, it was like working a mineral train at express speed.

I have never actually fired an N.B. Atlantic on one of these trains, but I have driven them often enough, and I could relive the experience with Bill when he recounted to me the details of that trip on No. 877 *Liddesdale*. I could imagine that engine "digging her toes in" as she took the strain of the load on starting from Dundee right on to a 1 in 70 gradient, with a curve to the Tay Bridge which about broke your heart even to look at, if you were an engineman.

There was no hope of finesse with this start away on the last lap to Edinburgh. It was sheer slogging. The reversing lever was left full out, the sand was running and the driver stood on an N.B. Atlantic bent away to the right with his arm at full stretch, his hand on a wide open throttle in case of a slip, his neck stretched to its limit in the opposite direction, keeping an eye on the signals, which more often than not were just dropping as he neared them. The blast from Bill's *Liddesdale* would have made the man-in-the-moon pick the cinders out of his eyes.

All the time he would be praying inwardly that none of those "stop boards" would remain "on," for to stop on that curving stretch with all those wheels behind you holding the rails like grim death meant a real battle to get moving again. Not until he was on the "straight" of the Bridge itself could he relax shut the sand and draw the lever up to stop the piled up fire being cleared from the "box" completely.

The slogging, however, wasn't over. For a good two miles the lever on an Atlantic was somewhere in the region of "four" or maybe "five," which in the modern fashion you can put at approximately 40/45 per cent. cut-off. And it remained there until near St. Fort, where the first downhill run commences.

If you ever get the chance of looking at a fish train running at high speed, try and get the view the driver obtains as he looks back from the cab. It isn't so bad nowadays with six-wheeled vans making for steady running, but it is impressive enough. In 1911, with an N.B. Atlantic to lend colour to the picture, it was really worth witnessing.

As I have said, there was nothing on rails which could pitch and roll like those engines, so that at high speed with a fish train, the spectacle was like a giant whip, with the engine as the stock, and the train acting the part of the lash as it belted round the curves, with water from the slowly melting ice in the fish boxes spurting from the vans in every direction. How these old fish vans kept the road is either a remarkable testimony to the N.B. surface-men or an abstruse matter of adhesion which defies application of any recognisable formula to explain it. To try and describe the total movements, all taking place at the one time on those trains during the curving downward swoop into Leuchars, is impossible.

Before you were round the Leuchars bend, the throttle was again wide open and you were away again and up to the level stretch, before tackling the enormous mountain which is Falkland bank. The top of Falkland is almost a "peak," where *Liddesdale* in seconds would reverse the direction in which her nose was pointing, and tear on her way downhill with unabated savagery.

At the foot of that bank was a 10mph slack, and it was here that you showed just how good (or bad) you were with the brake. Each of these vans had a braking system of democratic independence. No two of them went on with the same force or any desire for harmony, and some of them just pretended to go on. If the couplings stood up to it, and the train was all in one piece, you slipped quietly through the "hole" which was a subsiding Thornton, and "gave her the works" once more. Up another bank along a short level stretch and with a screaming, whistling, pitching roll downhill, *Liddesdale* would round the sharp left-hand bend which hides Kirkcaldy.

This is what Bill's engine was doing when she ploughed into a gang of surfacemen busy in the centre of the "four-foot." No engineman dwells on these moments, and Bill Stevenson is no exception. "There were no look-out men in those days, Norman," he commented briefly, and went on to tell about the Board of Trade inquiry which followed. It was that tragedy in 1911, Bill thinks, and a Board of Trade recommendation after the inquiry, which forced the N.B.R. to provide a look-out for permanent way men engaged on work on the line.

Now and again, I hear my mates cribbing at having to carry out the safety code embodied in the rule book. I've listened to passengers moaning at delays to trains in which they are travelling, and I think how these apparent frustrations were built up one by one, each a milestone of tragedy, through the long years of railway history. Then the moans and cribbings assume true value, and possibly I crack a joke rather than try to explain. That is what Bill did as he switched quickly on to the yarn about how he was oiling the Westinghouse brake cylinder of No. 596 and forgot to shut the connecting cock between the engine and the train to which she was coupled. At that moment the guard tested the brake from the back end. A great gusher of oil blackened Bill, as 70 pounds of compressed air shot it back through the hole into which he had just poured it. I laughed dutifully and was relieved to see the hard look fade out of his eyes.

Unlike mine, Bill's knees were fit to display under a kilt and he joined up in the "Dandy Ninth," the only kilted battalion of the Royal Scots. That phase of military glory didn't last long, however, He was more unlucky than I, and before he knew where he was, in 1915 was back on the footplate—but in a foreign land. From 1915 until 1918 he was driving almost everything on wheels between Abbeville and Armentieres—long trains hitched on to American Baldwins, or any other engines which could run the French miners to the coal mines near Armentieres.

It was real rough stuff, and he never knew from day to day just what was in store for him. Engines were running with almost everything missing except the pistons and driving wheels. They came from every railway company in Britain, and Bill Stevenson holds the distinction of driving the first Midland 0-6-0 which landed in France. Of the lot, he liked the N.B. 0-6-0 best, for a most peculiar reason—"the brake blocks didn't wear out so quickly as the others. We had an awful job getting blocks once they wore down, you know."

It was something he said about big driving wheels which reminded me of another tale and I broke in with a question. "By the way, Bill," I asked, "how long is it since you lost the driving tyre off *Windsor Lad,* and what's the real yarn about that bit of fun and games?"

I had never heard the rights of that episode, which if it had been written as fiction would never have been believed. Yet it actually happened on Gresley "A3" 4-6-2 No. 2500, as she was numbered when Bill Stevenson was driving her.

"Oh, that," said Bill, as if he was telling about a nice cup of tea he had once. "I never knew we lost that tyre until I got to the shed, and had time to look round her. It was on a return Sunday excursion from Newcastle. I was driving on the spare in 1930—I think. Old *Windsor Lad* was doing her stuff all right in 15 per cent. all the way, and it was a pretty wild night, dark with a real wind off the sea. Incidentally, she was a better 'A3' than your *Spearmint* ever was." (He just couldn't resist that "crack" and there was the usual digression while I put him wise as to the finest "A3" which ever came out of Doncaster.)

"We were about twenty-five miles from Edinburgh," he resumed. "The exact spot was Stenton Crossing, this side of Dunbar. I pulled the catch out of the lever to pull her up a wee bit, when the *'Lad'* gave a lurch, righted herself, and ran on as sweet as a nut. You know how it is when you are running at 70, as we were doing then; there's all sorts of little lurches you get, over in a flash, and quite unexplainable—maybe a bit of ballast on the rail, a rabbit, or some other thing, which registers but doesn't bother you.

"That's what happened that night. Then at Prestonpans the smell came floating back to the cab. When I shut off for the "easy" through Montonhall Junction, that smell registered far more than the wee lurch further back, and worried me a great deal more. You know how it was with our bunch on the spare—a heating box was a blot on the escutcheon.

"But I wasn't stopping. We were nearly home, so I sailed into the Waverley, and my mate coupled off. I had no time to leave the cab, as we had to clear out to let another engine tie on to take part of the train on to Glasgow. I set the engine on the turntable when we got to Haymarket and nipped down on the right side from where the smell of heating had been wafting. I didn't need to look; my nose took me straight to the right leading 'driver'. Was it hot? That box almost lifted the skin off my hand."

"Just then my mate, who had been looking round the left side, hollered out: 'She's lost a brake block on this side, Bill!' I went round to where he was standing at the left leading driving wheel. The block was gone all right. Then my lamp moved, and my eyes almost dropped out.

" 'A brake block lost! That's nothing—just look at this!' I shouted. I shoved the lamp up against the edge of the wheel—we'd lost a blinking tyre! I told him not to let anyone move her while I hurried off to the shed office. The 'gaffer' thought I was pulling his leg as usual, and firmly refused to believe me—that's the worst of kidding 'em on occasionally. But when he did realise it was true, the telephone wires almost became red-hot. To cut it short, when they searched the line they discovered that tyre away in the middle of a field. It was in two halves. One of the halves had sliced through a telegraph pole, and it and the wires were also lying in the field by the lineside. It's a good job they fell the right way or I and many more mightn't have been here to tell the tale."

I knew about that miraculous happening, but I had never got round to getting the details, and I think this is the first time the inside story has been told. Naturally I've heard of many, and in some cases actually experienced a few curious locomotive casualties where defects have developed, but I have always put this one down as the most fantastic I have come across. If ever the guiding hand of Providence was in evidence on a speeding engine it was on this occasion. The heating box on the other side, of course, was explained by the fact that the weight was thrown on to the right side by the loss of the left tyre, and no journal will stand that sort of thing.

If anyone had told me before this happened that a Gresley Pacific could run at high speed for twenty-five miles without her driver being aware that a leading tyre was missing, I just wouldn't have believed it, especially with a driver of the calibre of Bill Stevenson, who, over long years, has proved himself one of the most knowledgeable in the game. I've always said the Gresleys were good, but even I wouldn't have dared to say they were so good that they could run like a deer with only five driving wheels on the rail.

Bill's regular engine was a Gresley "A4" streamliner, No. 60027 *Merlin*. Like all drivers on the top link at Haymarket he's had that engine for quite a *few* years, and I hope to tell the story of how we came to get regular engines in a later chapter. He thinks there's nothing quite like "27" anywhere on earth, but he's quite wrong of course. I can tell him of a better engine; and Jim Swan, my particular "butty," can do the same, but Jim won't mean the same "better" engine. In point of fact the bunch of us who became "possessors" of Gresleys went slightly haywire on the care, maintenance and sheer devotion we lavished on these "horses" of ours. But they were worth it.

Bill is a good hand, good enough to have had members of the Royal Family travelling behind his engine on nine occasions: good enough to knock spots off the timing of trains like the "Capitals Limited," "Elizabethan," and their like when it's needed. One of these occasions may be quoted to show the manner of his approach to the much debated question of "should a driver regain time?"

It was on a down run of the "Capitals Limited" in 1950. Bill had taken over the engine from York as usual, after a trip from London which hadn't been too good from a running point of view. Signal checks had cramped the style considerably, and the train was about 10 minutes behind time. To Bill, this wasn't anything to worry over. He'd pick that back with ease before reaching Edinburgh, but he reckoned without fate and other impedimenta to fast running. From one cause or another all the way from York to Berwick, just when he was pulling the minutes back, another signal check kept him behind time. When he crossed the Border Bridge at Berwick he was still running late.

Even yet, with a sustained "bash" and a ruthless abuse of a willing engine, he could have hammered off those lost minutes, but "bashing" isn't Bill's way.

"It's no good hammering until you heat up a 'box' or a big-end to regain a few minutes, and have the engine laid up for days out of traffic," he said, "but at the same time I wanted to knock off that time. So I put her into 15 per cent., gave her just that little extra with the throttle which not only pulled the time back in *seconds* spun out over the entire sixty miles, and kept her just on the right side of starting a 'heat,' but kept within every speed restriction to a hair's-breadth. We did the last sixty miles in fifty-two minutes."

That is his terse description of a really fine feat of enginemanship, which perhaps only an engineman could appreciate. Anyone can "bash on regardless" and regain time, but it isn't everyone who can do it and look his engine in the face at the end of the trip, conscience-clear that he has given her a fair deal.

In his early days on *Merlin* the officers of the naval aircraft repair depot at Donibristle often travelled in the Aberdeen train which Bill worked with "27." This aircraft depot was known in the Admiralty records as H.M.S. *Merlin* and those Navy men were keenly interested in the way Bill and his engine handled the train. So these sailors got together, and one day the two *Merlins* met. Bill's engine, shining even more than usual, was wangled over rails

Andrew Manzie with No. 423 of the N.B. "420" class, taken about 1900.

Locomotive Foreman
Jim Lawrie, Haymarket
Shed, about 1910.

Close-up of cab controls
of N.B. 18 in. cylinder
goods 0-6-0. Note the
"tallow" kettle on the
flame plate and old-
fashioned lubricator for
the valves.

N.B. 4-4-0 tank No. 98, which used to run between Dalmeny and Edinburgh.

N.B. 18 in. cylinder 0-6-0 goods locomotive *Allenby* (L.N.E. No. 9611). Locomotives of this class which served overseas during the 1914-18 war were given names.

The smallest type on the N.B.R., an 0-4-0 saddle tank for dock and yard shunting.

No. 731 of the N.B. "730" class 4-4-0s. The immaculate condition typifies the way in which locomotives were kept before the 1914-18 war. *Locomotive Publishing Co.*

"Glen" class 4-4-0 N.B. No. 270 *Glen Garry.* Note name below smokebox door as well as on splasher. The author fired on the first run of this engine on the "Fife Coast Express"'. *R.D. Stephen*

N.B. Atlantic *Bon-Accord* (L.N.E. No. 9870) heads a southbound express out of Aberdeen Joint Station. *Locomotive Publishing Co.*

N.B. Atlantic No. 878 *Hazeldean*. This engine, driven by Tom Henderson of Haymarket, took part in a trial with the North Eastern Atlantics.
Locomotive Publishing Co.

Edinburgh Waverley Station in the late North British days. *Locomotive Publishing Co.*

North Eastern "Z" class Atlantic (L.N.E. No. 717). *Locomotive Publishing Co.*

N.E. "Z" class Atlantic No. 727 as rebuilt in 1931 with booster and articulated tender. *British Railways*

Gresley "P2" 2-8-2 No. 2001 *Cock o' the North*. Note the distinctive fore-end, which had a camshaft and poppet valves. This class was rebuilt to the Pacific wheel arrangement. *E.R. Wethersett*

2-8-2 No. 2002 *Earl Marischal* on the 1.40pm fish train passing Ferryhill Junction, Aberdeen. This "P2" class was designed by Gresley specially for the Edinburgh-Aberdeen line. *C. Lawson Kerr*

Great Eastern Holden class "B12" 4-6-0 with the prominent feed water apparatus which led to their being dubbed "Hikers". The LNER subsequently drafted engines of this class to Scotland.

"V4" class 2-6-2 No. 61700 *Bantam Cock* on an Aberdeen-Edinburgh fish train near Cove Bay. *C. Lawson Kerr*

Ross Dougan (on the left) with No. 4472 *Flying Scotsman*, the first locomotive to run non-stop from Edinburgh to London.

"A3" No. 2796 *Spearmint* at Kings Cross after working the non-stop *Flying Scotsman. W.J. Reynolds*

No. 60100 *Spearmint* passing Reston with the 1.25pm out of Waverley. *G. Ogilvie*

The "Coronation", headed by Gresley "A4" No. 2512 *Silver Fox* with original full streamlining and blue livery. *C.L. Turner*

A4 4-6-2 No. 60030 *Golden Fleece* at Haymarket ready to work the southbound "Elizabethan". Driver Jim Swan (also inset) discusses the trip with his opposite number who will take over after Tollerton, north of York. *Locomotive Express Ltd.*

The author (seated, right) with a group of locomotive enthusiasts in Edinburgh, 1953. Standing, left to right, are Peter Fraser, driver, Corkerhill; Len Y. Pile, top link driver, Camden; W. McGowan Gradon; John Drayton, driver, Pontypool. With the author is Jim Swan, top link driver, Haymarket. *N. McKillop*

Above: Tommy Smith of Haymarket in the cab of "A4" No. 60031 *Golden Plover. British Railways*

Left: Bill Stevenson of Haymarket looks out of the cab window of "A4" No. 60027 *Merlin. British Railways*

where nothing more than a freight engine had passed, and stood in splendid majesty inside the aircraft depot.

There Bill with his opposite number Bob Keppie, their firemen, and a company of locomotive officers and others, gathered to witness a ceremony which must be unique in Scottish railway history.

Mr. B. P. Blackburn, our District Superintendent, accepted from the Commandant of *Merlin,* the depot, two cast brass plaques made there. The plaques were enamelled in colour, and showed in relief that beautiful bird, the merlin, in full flight over the sea. Those works of art still adorn each side of the boiler of "27" as a lasting tribute to a grand engine and an equally grand crew.

After the formalities it was a real day out as only the Navy can lay on. We were all dined superbly and did the rounds of the depot with fellows who not only knew their stuff but had such a friendly and humorous way of putting it over, that what would have been a monotonous monologue became a joyous occasion right up to the biggest highlight of the day, when Bill and others of us found ourselves away up in the sky in a plane specially laid on. When we landed after flying over the sea and the Perthshire hills, it was difficult to tear those pilots and ourselves apart. We swapped yarns on our different experiences, and Bill took them over *Merlin* the locomotive—on which, incidentally, the German airmen had concentrated their attention one night as he came up the east coast.

At the time I was writing this, Bill retired, and on his last run the B.B.C. came along and broadcast a commentary on his footplate career. At least, that was the intention. I didn't hear the broadcast, but from what I can gather, Bill, very adroitly as is his habit, spoke more about *Merlin* which he was driving for the last time, than about his footplate record. He passed on from that to what he intended to do in his garden, and how he was going to at last see his favourite football team, Heart of Midlothian, every week instead of no more than occasionally.

He came to me the week before I wrote this chapter, still as tough, still hardly a grey hair in his plentiful thatch, and still as young as ever. "How's the garden getting on Bill?" I asked. "Garden! I've no time for gardening," he grinned. "I'm driving the strongest 'pug' in Edinburgh for so-and-so. The B.R. tanky in the yard just can't cope with the wagons we haul to her and she has two more wheels than my engine."

I grinned all over. I knew that would happen. He would have told me in five minutes she was better than my Gresley *Spearmint* if I'd let him carry on.

Life With "Swannie"

I once read a description of a "typical engine driver," and was so tickled that I wrote a song to the tune of the *British Grenadiers,* which was sung with great gusto at our social gatherings away back in 1919. It started off:

"For some of us are big and fat

And some of us are short and squat

In the Loco Engineers, the Loco Engineers ...

That "typical" stuff is all nonsense, of course, but if there could be a "typical" engineman I think he would be fashioned like "Swannie," my particular "butty" at Haymarket. Five foot six in his socks, stocky and strong as they make 'em, he is an ideal inside-right at football and no mean exponent with a pair of boxing gloves. A pawky wit and a sense of humour make him grand company, and he is as forthright in expressing his opinions as anyone on two feet.

One of these opinions is "that anything above five feet six is wasted in the cab of a railway engine." As I'm slightly more than that I took pleasure in proving him wrong as often as I could. Another of his opinions is that there is nothing on wheels to touch his Gresley streamliner *William Whitelaw;* this, too, is a fallacy, of course, which *Spearmint* and I proved over and over again. In fact the way he had that engine of his tricked out made me tell him once it wasn't a real engine at all—just a big "pansy" amongst honest-to-goodness engines like the Gresley "A3s."

Jim spent most of his waking moments thinking up ideas on how to improve the detail refinements in the cab, quite apart from having it shining like a jeweller's window. Every minute that engine stood there was always some job to do until every control worked with such smooth ease, that I used to swear they made you languid even to think of them. That's the kind of engineman he was.

Like myself Jim went through the mill at Haymarket in his early days. For his sins he too became the slave of "Shorty" in the yard, and like me hated that grease box and all it stood for. Unlike me, however, he did some very real firing and needed all the muscle he possessed to stand the hefty spell he put in at the end of a shovel on 874, and 876, the Atlantics on which he fired regularly to John Sinclair and Tom Henderson on the Aberdeen runs.

His first trip with Henderson wasn't a happy one. The coal was so dirty that it not only filled the firebox to the brick arch with dirt, but on the return trip the tender was stripped bare. All 11 tons of coal was burned, and at Dundee, still with 60 miles to go, another engine was set up alongside 876, with a gang shovelling the coal on to the Atlantic tender like mad to allow her to carry on.

"Good old days," said Swannie, grinning when he told me about it recently.

Another of Jim's experiences which missed me, was the Milngavie (pronounced Mulguy) and Clydebank lodging turns. These places are a mere fifty odd miles from Edinburgh, yet there was a regular link which lodged away from home every second night, and all the extra they got for this was 3s. a night. After doing the trip from Edinburgh they spent the rest of their day making short trips round a number of little stations in and around Glasgow, then remained there to work back in the next morning.

Three shillings for lodgings didn't mean many frills or glossy surroundings for the chaps with only that to spend, and their landladies went in for economies, one of which was that two should share one bed. Nobody thought anything about that and the powers-that-be would have considered it downright uppishness on a driver or fireman's part if they had protested.

In point of fact, some of the drivers considered it slightly degrading to be asked to sleep with a fireman, and insisted they occupy a bed with men of their own caste, the fireman to sleep with his own lower orders. Jim's mate, however, was more democratic, and apart from demanding precedence at the washing bowl, acted more or less like a human being. So Jim lay in bed with the exalted. That is until he kicked the exalted one out the first night under the impression he was saving his life.

That first night young Swan woke up with the smell of burning in his nostrils. The bed was on fire—at least the smoke was pouring all round his head. Without stopping to think, still half asleep (Jim was always prompt in emergencies) and before getting out of danger himself, he got both his feet into the bulk of his driver's back, shot him out of bed, then leaped for safety himself. Then he realised his *faux pas;* the bed wasn't on fire at all, it was only his driver having a smoke.

Jim Swan wasn't meant to come into the footplate grades. The "parents," says he, "maybe intended me to be a scientist, for I spent my early years in the laboratory of the University of Edinburgh." But you might as well have tried to stop Niagara as try to stop the urge that was running through Jim Swan's blood stream to become an engine driver.

John Sinclair, to whom he eventually fired on 874, was his uncle, while his family tree is cluttered with railwaymen of one kind or another. Even his father, an engineer, served on the railways for some time. So Jim Swan just couldn't help it; he Was a "natural" for life on the footplate if ever there was one.

Although he was senior to me, the advent of the eight hours' day started us both driving in 1919, and from that moment, while bosom pals, the battle was on. Each of us was determined that "anything you can do I can do better," which meant occasionally 'ploys' quite without the officially known and accepted conduct of engine drivers in the course of their duty. Yet, while Swannie and I could and did play many a prank, there was never any question of how seriously we regarded our responsibilities as enginemen, nor of the manner in which we carried them out. So don't, repeat *don't,* take what follows as an example, or in any way typical, of life on the footplate.

I have mentioned the Class "S" 0-6-0 and how I worked one on a goods to Glasgow without using the brake. Naturally, both my mate and I had to do a spot of bragging about this to Swannie and his mate.

"Och, that's nothing," said Jim, "tell him what we do, mate." And his mate (about as daft as himself), having pronounced that working without using the brake was mere child's play, claimed that they worked their train without being on the engine at all.

"All right," I said, "I'll buy it, tell me what foolishness you've been up to." And I got the yarn.

"Well, I never liked that signalman at so-and-so," said Jim. "You know how he stands in the box waving a lamp outside his window telling you to hurry up, although you're running dead on your schedule. I don't mind that occasionally, but he makes a habit of it.

"One dark morning my mate and I jammed ourselves into the corner of the cab, and when the old 'S' passed that rubber-necking old nuisance his eyes almost fell out. For all he could see there wasn't a driver or fireman on the engine. We watched him making a dash for his bells and could almost hear him giving the runaway signal to the man in the box ahead. We were stopping there anyway so no harm was being done. When we drew up at the next box we exchanged civilities as usual with the signalman, who was giving us long looks, but he didn't give his pal away. But he *was* very busy on the telephone, and I could guess what all the conversation was about. So just ask that lad at so-and-so; he'll bear me out that when it's my turn on the 'Cadder' the train doesn't need a driver or fireman."

That set me thinking.

"Look," I said to my mate Geordie Lister, the next time we were on that job, "we'll arrange a performance of our own for that signalman."

Geordie was six foot of sheer devilment. "We'll stage him a major thrill in the best American style," he suggested. "Tomorrow morning you'll be on your knees when we pass that box and I'll be choking the life out of you."

"To the devil with that," I said. "If there's to be anybody choking anybody else, then as the driver I'm claiming the right to do the choking."

Actually I had forgotten all about Geordie's fertile imagination ten minutes after the conversation, and certainly the next morning when we came up to the signalbox I wasn't even thinking of putting on a sideshow. It was only when I saw the signalman almost fall out of the box pointing to the tender that I realised George wasn't going to be done out of his dramatic act. There he was, sprawled full out on his back on the coal, the whole six feet of him, his face contorted, his cap lying some distance away and the coal hammer ostentatiously displayed, for all the world as if someone had clouted him over the head.

For a single moment I almost believed it myself, until I saw the grin on his face. "Come down out of that, you young ass," I shouted. "Swannie and you will drive that chap nuts!" I tried to look serious, but it was a failure.

We were "lifting and leaving" at the next box, and when we stopped, the signalman was full of concern for Geordie, who was on his side of the cab. The bare-faced way that lad told a pack of "terminological inexactitudes" was a tribute to his acting ability. With a face as grave as a judge he sent back all sorts of sympathetic messages to the fellow in the other box, to the effect that he also suffered with his eyes, and that the signalman would do well to "bathe them three times a day with a boracic solution and he'd soon be all right."

He really wasn't a bad lad, that signalman whose leg we were pulling—just anxious to get on with the job. I thought we ought to let him know the story of his "hallucinations" months later, when we were stopped at his box by some impediment ahead. He joined in the laugh, and every time Jimmy or I passed his box after that, he would hold up a hammer and wave, which rather puzzled a colleague of mine who was learning the road with me.

"What's he holding up the hammer for?" he asked.

"Oh," says the nonchalant Geordie, "my driver and he and I are members of a secret society devoted to murder. The signalman kills his victims with that hammer, and we burn them in the firebox. The perfect crime, laddie."

My colleague looked a bit shocked. In those days the cult of the "whodunits" hadn't reached the stage it has nowadays, with two or three violent deaths in the first chapter as tip-top reading entertainment. Geordie was certainly ahead of his time, and that's maybe why he left the service for something more in keeping with his imagination and acting ability.

Don't imagine from the foregoing that life with "Swannie" on the footplate was one big laugh. Like all of his breed he knew when the joke was over, and while he never allowed his job of high-speed train running to become a soul-devouring business to the exclusion of every other human desire, he has given it sufficient of himself to have become, in my opinion, one of the finest enginemen in the game.

Neither am I alone in this thought. Just prior to writing this chapter I had a chat with Ted Hailstone of Kings Cross, who mated Jim for seven years on the "Capitals Limited" and the "Elizabethan", the Edinburgh-London nonstop. Ted told me "Jim wasn't only a great engineman, he was a great mate and a man as well,", and that's no mean tribute from a fellow who takes over an engine from a colleague after it has done nearly 200 miles of hard running, and still has the same distance to do before the trip is over.

Jim Swan and I were talking recently at the best of all places, his "ain fireside", and our talk was of high-speed trains and how to run them.

"What about that record run you did with 60034 on the 'Elizabethan,' in 1952" I asked him. "You know the one I mean; it was logged by A. S. Haddon and included in an article by our old friend Cecil J. Allen in *The Railway Magazine.*"

"Funnily enough, that wasn't the hard slogging run you might have imagined; at least, it wasn't nearly as difficult as many of the other runs I've experienced on that same train," said Jim. "As far as I can recollect we did the 124½ miles from Newcastle to Edinburgh in under 114 minutes, and regained nearly sixteen minutes of the twenty minutes lost between London and Newcastle.

"It was a lousy trip right from the start. There was a series of signal checks from Kings Cross to York, every time the Kings Cross lads were getting back the time. You know how it happens— a check by signals, a few minutes lost and you have it all mapped out where you are going to step on it and regain the time. It all works out nicely; then 'wham'—a 'distant' steadies you up right on the worst bit, and again you're down.

"This went on the whole road to York, where I took over. We actually passed York 17 down, and believe me it wouldn't have been out of place if another ten minutes had been added to that, for these Kings Cross men had certainly been doing their darnedest to cut the losses."

"Between York and Newcastle it was just as bad, and by that time I was wondering if they had mistaken the 'Elizabethan' for a coal train, the way we were being tied up. Not only that, but on a train like the 'Elizabethan' all those signal checks meant that we were burning a lot more coal and using a great deal more water than normally, and you know how I hated to stop that 'nonstop'."

"If '34' hadn't been the engine she was, I'm certain we couldn't have done that trip as easily as we did. She was riding as smoothly as a carriage, and her coal and water consumption was just nothing at all. So when we cleared Newcastle, we were in good trim, all of us, to hit the high spots. That is, if we were allowed to," Jim added.

"Right now I'd like to say that Davy Booth, my fireman, deserved a lot of credit for that performance. From first to last he gave me the real hot steam without which the trip could never have been run as it was.

"You know how you can read the signs when a train ahead has stopped, restricting your running," Jim went on. "On each section from York I had been doing the usual thing to find out. On each long section I had been accelerating a great deal more quickly than usual, and each time the distant told me that the train ahead was still keeping me back.

"But by the time I got on to the King Edward Bridge before Newcastle, I knew from the signs that we were free of the restriction which had cramped our style from York. I had a look at the water level in the tank (we had plenty of coal on the tender), and Davy didn't even need to be told what was going to happen.

"All the distants were lying off for us, and once we were through the 25mph slack at the 'Manors' I wasted no time. We were off. For the first time since York, I shoved the reverser into 23 per cent, and that took us nicely through Heaton at the required 40, but before that I let '34' out a nick and we were sailing up that 1 in 200 to Forest Hall as if it were level."

"It's five miles to Forest Hall, and under normal running I took something like ten minutes to do this section, not only because of the gradient but, as you know, you've got to be mighty careful on the restrictions at Manors and Heaton. Instead of ten we passed Forest Hall in just under eight minutes and by that time '34' was in 20 per cent. and full throttle.

"By Cramlington, still in 20 per cent. we were doing over 60, and that isn't so bad—it's a 'sticky' section, that is. It looks easy, but whether it's the road-bed or no, it's not as simple as it looks. Even here '34' was showing me what she really could do, so much so that I had her pulled up into 15 per cent. a long way from Stannington, where we were doing over 80 before I shut off and let the speed peter out before braking for the 40mph slack on the curve at Morpeth.

"We were just doing 40 at Morpeth," said Swannie, "for that's one of the places where the engineer is dead right in imposing a limit, although I don't always agree with him in all he does," he added with a grin. "Anyway," he continued, "we had pinched back two of these twenty minutes, which wasn't so bad on that difficult stretch. I gave '34' her head out of Morpeth and a good 30 per cent. to start off with. In no time at all we were in the 60's, and by the time Longhirst was passed we were heading for 70, and the reverser was back in 15 per cent. for quite a while. We were through the dip at Alnmouth, 34 miles from Newcastle, in thirty-four minutes. To do that we were running at 80mph quite often, if you consider the restrictions on those first 34 miles.

"It's five miles of mostly 1 in 190 up the curving bank between Alnmouth and Little Mill, and we did that on the full throttle and no more than 25 per cent. Mark you, from start to finish of the trip never once was the second injector used to fill up the boiler. I had to watch that, even if that Gresley was as easy as they make 'em. We did that five miles of bank in four minutes, yet we could have done it more quickly if I'd been prepared to flog the engine unmercifully.

"On the eight miles down or so of Christon Bank we were doing well over the 85mph with just as much steam being used as would work the exhaust injector, and the lever in just under 15 per cent. We passed Lucker, steadied up to take water at the troughs, and were through Belford sixteen instead of twenty minutes down. And '34' was still doing it on under 1 per cent. and using little more than 'drift' steam.

"It wasn't the engine which restricted us now in running faster, it was the road, and, quite frankly, I could have run a lot harder on this stretch if the engineer would have allowed it. By the time we got to Berwick I knew it was in the bag and was quite confident I could have arrived in Edinburgh on time. The way that engine was running up the banks with over 400 tons of train behind her told me a lot. We actually did the climb of 2½ miles between Goswick and Scremerston at over 70mph with the reverser never further out than 20 per cent.; and that bank is mostly 1 in 190.

"We passed Berwick in just one hour—not bad considering the restrictions, and the uphill bits on this nearly 66 miles. Up to now we had pulled back six minutes of the lost time. I don't need to tell you how you make up time between Berwick and Edinburgh. Mostly it's done on the long climbs, and on this last stretch I had as much in the way of coal and water as to warrant me giving '34' a good deal more of her own way than she'd had up to now.

"So, before we cleared the Berwick platform at the required 30mph, the throttle was wide open and the reverser (if I mind rightly) was as far down as 35 per cent. And I left it there for a few minutes although the cracks that were coming from that engine could be heard for miles. We cleared Grantshouse a minute to the good, and this was done mostly in 25 per cent. after the initial start on this 15 miles of largely 1 in 190/200 up. Then it was easy all the way in.

"I believe we did an average of 80 for thirty miles, which means 90 down Co'path and a lot of 80's and over here and there. But I might have known that sort of thing just doesn't earn a play-back. In spite of all I had done in regaining time, when Edinburgh hove in sight, with me all set to arrive on time, blest if we weren't steadied by signals at Joppa—so that was that.

"Instead of knocking off that 20 minutes we arrived four minutes late, which may have been considered a good enough performance, but to me it was spoiled by that check at Joppa, which 'put the peter on' my plan. I'd no more chance of recovering time, which maybe accounts for my refusal to consider the run very outstanding even if it was a record of sorts."

It was the mention by Jim of his "plan" for running, which recalled another of his "plans" that created a world record. I didn't need him to give me the details. We had discussed it often enough, and I think no account of Haymarket men would be complete without its inclusion. It has been published before, but this is the first time the inside story has been told of how the longest non-stop run was "planned". Possibly all my readers know the yarn. However, for those not acquainted with the facts it may be better to state them.

Jim Swan was working the "Flying Scotsman" during September 1948 when it was scheduled to run non-stop between Edinburgh and London. That is, it would have been non-stop if one of the most spectacular happenings in Scottish railway history had not taken place. In August, flooding took place to such an extent on the main East Coast route that a section of the line was completely cut off from Dunbar to Berwick, a distance of nearly 30 miles.

Overnight, bridges were swept away, leaving the rails hanging in mid air. Huge lakes formed which threatened to wash away railway embankments, and in one case, so serious was this that the folk in a low-lying village had to be warned of their danger in case the piled-up masses of water should breach the embankment and descend upon them in a rushing torrent.

In all this destruction and potential danger, not one casualty occurred, not one wheel was derailed, and I feel that if it has never been stated before in any account of this major happening it should be stated now, that the hand of Providence was very evident in its guidance on this occasion.

All the Edinburgh and London East Coast trains were diverted via the Waverley route of the former North British, including, of course, Jim Swan's "non-stop" "Flying Scotsman," and to those who don't know, this route is an entirely different road from the East Coast. To get to Tweedmouth and so rejoin the East Coast route it was necessary to climb Falahill some 8½ miles of twisting long up-gradients mostly at 1 in 70. Then comes a long downward run to Galashiels, followed by a rigidly speed-restricted single line to Kelso and thence a branch line to Tweedmouth. From Galashiels running was restricted to no more than 25mph for Pacific engines.

Instructions were issued to the non-stop drivers that in view of the load (465 tons) it would be necessary *(a)* to stop for a pilot to assist in rear between Hardengreen and Falahill, and *(b)* in view of the increased distance between Edinburgh and the water troughs at Lucker (now 92 instead of 76 miles away by the direct route), to stop for water at either Galashiels or Tweedmouth.

This is how things were when Jim Swan decided to "make a plan," firstly because it irked his soul that the much publicised "non-stop" should have to stop, and secondly, because he felt that the Gresley Pacific was capable of doing what it eventually did do. I think everyone knows what happened on September 7, 1948. The "Flying Scotsman" with Gresley "A4" No. 60029 *Woodcock* at the head, passed Hardengreen at full belt, climbed Falahill, sauntered past Galashiels, *and* Tweedmouth, picked up 4,500 gallons of water at Lucker troughs and went on to create the longest non-stop run record, a distance of 408½ miles, against that of the L.M.S. Euston-Glasgow record of 401 miles set up by "Royal Scot" No. 6113 *Cameronian* in 1928.

These are the bald details as outlined in most of the accounts; now for the "plan" often enough discussed between Jim Swan and myself. Jim knew that the big snag to what he proposed to do, was the possibility either of being stopped by signals on Falahill, or of being unable to climb the hill. In either case he would be in a jam, for if once stopped on the face of that 1 in 70 gradient with 465 tons he wouldn't be able to start again without assistance. About water he had no qualms. Both he and I had regularly run the full 124½ miles between Edinburgh and Newcastle without bothering to lift water at Lucker, and still had 1,000 gallons left out of the 5,000 our Gresley tanks carried.

So, prior to his first attempt, Jim was taking careful notes. Testing the Pacific with the pilot behind him, he was quite satisfied that there was plenty of power in hand to take the "Flying Scotsman" up the hill. So far so good, but what he could not foresee was the possibility of being stopped and a lot of delay ensuing to this most important of all trains. That was a risk for which he would be held responsible.

So he carefully noted all the points where freight trains were shunted to allow his train passage, and after working it all out, came to the conclusion that if he had to stop on any part of the hill there would be a sufficient number of engines at strategic points to assist with no more delay to the train than would have taken place if he had stopped at Hardengreen for a pilot. Moreover, the time saved by not stopping for assistance or water was going to allow him to work the engine so much more easily that, as he said after it was done, "it was nae bother at all."

He declares that it wasn't really a difficult performance for the Gresley. "We were never out further than 35 per cent. the whole of the way up, and did the Falahill climb and non-stop run quite a few times after that initial run," he told me. That indicates just what kind of engineman is Jim Swan.

I have expanded rather fully on two of my colleagues and their doings with the Gresley Pacifies. I have done so to show that the "prophet isn't always without honour in his own country." But both Jim Swan and Bill Stevenson would be the first to protest that they are no more entitled to be singled out than a round dozen or so of their mates—not forgetting the lads who come from Kings Cross and with whom they have worked for so many years, in close harmony in running this non-stop Edinburgh-London express, whether it's been the "Flying Scotsman", "Capitals Limited" or the "Elizabethan." So in a further brief chapter or two I'd like to introduce you to a few of the others and briefly sketch some of the highlights attached to their names.

XI
Speed Merchants All

It was after I had my chat with "Swannie," that I decided it was time I had a get-together with Ted Hailstone of Kings Cross. Both of these lads have formed a sort of mutual admiration society composed of each other. This is really a significant thing, much more significant than is indicated in the social friendship. For the basis of their admiration is built upon seven years of working together as drivers on the same train. Seven years ago it was named the "Capitals Limited" and is now the "Elizabethan." To both of them it is simply the "non-stop."

It so happens that there are twelve drivers in each of the top links at Kings Cross and Haymarket, and Jim Swan and Ted Hailstone were tied to the same rostered spell, Jim to work the Edinburgh-York part of the non-stop run, Ted doing the job south of York (or rather from Tollerton, just north of York.)

I'm open to correction, but I believe there's no harder test for two human beings to go through and retain their respect and friendship than that of mating each other on the one engine, and the fact that both Jim Swan and Ted Hailstone can wax enthusiastic about each other after seven years of this contact is a significant commentary on the men and their ability.

So Ted and I spent an evening in London chatting mainly on the high speed running of railway trains and the tricks of the trade which make it possible. I wasn't long in Ted's company before I found that like "Swannie" he worked to a plan, but before going on to illustrate this let me do the introductions properly.

Ted Hailstone has even more excuse than Jim Swan for becoming an engine driver, but he is the exact opposite to Jim in physical appearance. Ted's grandfather drove locomotives on the Manchester Sheffield, & Lincolnshire Railway in the pioneering days. His father was a driver on the Midland, and his uncle drove the engines of the North Eastern for many years. Railway engines were his natural conversation, thoughts, and mental food from his earliest thinking moments.

Ted is big and burly with shoulders like an ox, slow talking with a quiet humour. In fact, the man quite belies the history of "hell-for-leather" runs attached to his name. Like myself, he started his footplate career inside locomotive fireboxes, becoming a "bar-boy," with the job of renewing the fire bars in fireboxes at Gorton Shed on the Great Central at the age of 14. Driving since 1920, first at Gorton, and then at Kings Cross since 1927, he has (up to the time of his retirement in April, 1957) been working top link express trains for eleven years.

Ted's regular engine, 60014 *Silver Link,* is one of the original "Silver Jubilee" breed, and this alone gave me a talking point. For away back in the days when they were doing their superb high-speed act on that fabulous train, I drove that engine some 200 miles, on one part of which I ran the highest speed I've ever achieved on a railway locomotive.

So we talked, Ted and I, and he told me a curious thing about consistency in running which gives another clue to the character of Driver Jim Swan. As I've already said, Jim and Ted mated each other on the non-stop. They got to know each other's working so well that Ted declares that if by any chance he did not get the usual supply of water at the troughs, he knew just how many gallons "Swannie" could do with at a pinch, to carry him to the next troughs when they changed over at Tollerton on the down run.

We talked of the "regular engine" and what it meant to the driver of highspeed trains. Ted summed it all up in one brief sentence. "In 1954/55, Norman," he said, " '14' went into the shops for a works overhaul with 112,000 miles of hard running behind her, and in all those miles she never once, on any one bearing, showed the slightest sign of heat.

"Mind you, I did not coddle her," he continued. As an example of what he meant he told me the yarn about the "Very Important Person" who came up to the cab one day just prior to the start of a trip. "Look, Ted," said the V.I.P., "my friend and I have been having a discussion about the maximum speed your engine can attain at Stoke Summit, and we've agreed that no more than 65mph could be got at the top."

Ted finalised the yarn tersely. *"Silver Link* was doing 80 at Essendine, and passed Stoke Summit at 70, but I *had* to get 80 at Essendine to do that," he said.

That showed me how Ted worked to a plan. I could see that flashing 80 at the exact moment it was needed, and I could visualise the gradual "opening out" with the reverser to hold the speed to the limit as that up gradient took a hand in trying to kill the speed. Also could I see the exact judgment with which he assessed the effect of the gradient, the length of it, and the time it would take to reduce that 80 to 70mph

I could *see* the steam chest pressure gauge telling him just how effectively the steam was doing the job, and I could *feel* the responses of "14" every bit of that speed climb. I could hear "14" telling Ted in no uncertain fashion just where and when to supply the little extra boost with the reverser, to hit the top of Stoke with 5mph more than the V.I.P. had thought the limit.

This induced me to put to Ted the question to which I've asked all the Gresley high-speed drivers I know. "Do you think that the 126mph of *Mallard* was the utmost the 'Gresleys' could have accomplished in their prime?" Ted's reply was typical of the driver who "owns" a regular Gresley "A4" streamlined Pacific locomotive. "I had the chance of getting *Mallard* as a regular engine" he said, "but preferred *Silver Link.* I believe, given the same conditions, she could have made records too." Having once or twice driven *Mallard* as well as *Silver Link* I'm not sure that I could disagree with him.

Like a good many of his breed, Ted Hailstone's exploits on the footplate brought him other experiences. One of them is worth recounting before finishing this brief picture of an outstanding engineman. One of the many people who were interested in Ted's record, and who had ridden in the trains he drove regularly, was an admiral of the Royal Navy. He had often had a chat with Ted at the beginning or the end of a trip. During one of these he suddenly said: "Oh, by the way, Ted, I've been with you when you were doing your job; how would you like to come with me and see part of mine? What about coming on an exercise on one of my submarines?" So on a certain day Ted was flown from London to a naval port, where the commander of one of the latest type of submarines not only made him welcome, but attached to him a junior officer to see he got all the "gen" plus the thrills. For twenty-eight hours Ted experienced what it is like to go into battle on a submarine.

It seems too, that high-speed engine driving is good training for life on the "subs," for to all the questions about how he felt as that submarine ploughed through or under the waves Ted's reply was "fine." Apparently the first time out on one of these under-water craft all sorts of unusual physical symptoms are supposed to make themselves manifest, but Ted Hailstone just didn't register any of them.

I've already said that the Navy man and the engineman are kindred spirits. Bill Stevenson went up into the clouds as a result of that kindred feeling. Ted Hailstone went below the surface of the sea; but there is another case which I'd like to quote where this kinship was made evident, before I desert the subject.

One of my colleagues in the top link at Haymarket is Bill MacLeod, a Gaelic-speaking Highlander. Bill likes wearing the kilt (not on the footplate, of course) and is, (or rather was) a prominent member of the Scots Greys concert party. Bill's songs, both English and Gaelic, were a top feature, while his monologues brought you up tense in your seat. If Bill hadn't been tied firmly by inclination to his Gresley streamliner he would have "hit the neons" in any theatre you care to think up.

Like most of the Highlanders he had a natural flair for the dramatic, and again like the majority of his countrymen he had a perfect speaking voice (which, incidentally, very nearly made him a film actor, but I'll tell how that came about later).

Bill's engine was No. 60024, *Kingfisher* and while it was seen often enough on the Edinburgh-London expresses, it (and Bill) did quite a bit of running on the Glasgow, Perth, and Aberdeen trains, as light relief to the mileage turns on the East Coast. On the Aberdeen trains a naval officer got "pally" and interested. He was not only a naval officer, he was also an artist of some ability, and to show his admiration for both *Kingfisher* and Bill, he designed and cast two bronze plaques, enamelled them in the natural colours of the gorgeous bird after which Bill's Gresley was named, and got permission to have them affixed to the engine boiler. Not satisfied with this he painted Bill sitting in the cab, and I'm wondering if this is the only occasion that a Gresley driver has been so painted. Bill has that oil painting to this day and thinks a lot of it. Yes, the enginemen of today thinks the Navy of today's "all right."

But apart from the Royal Navy it is perhaps natural that the high-speed engine driver should attract a lot of attention from this and that source, and that's how it came about that Bill Macleod spent a week or two as a "film star."

A locomotive sequence was required for a film story, so Haymarket became a welter of flood lighting, cinema technicians were almost as numerous as the total staff at the depot, with Bill and his engine making their entrances and exits to the manner born. They took shots of the engine with the relief cocks blowing full bore, shots with the cocks shut, shots where she was moving with nothing but the Gresley "knock" to be heard, and shots with everything on tap, safety valves, whistle, and blast (with plenty of smoke, of course). Bill was so successful that the sequence was extended and Bill and his "pin-up" fireman went through quite a "spiel" of drama. They were highly complimented on their natural ability for the screen. Incidentally, Bill's fireman had all that it takes for that sort of work, but he couldn't have cared less—and that goes for Bill as well.

Neither could Tony MacLeod, who with Bill drove *Kingfisher* on the opposite shift. Tony is a great, six-foot-two Highlander from the same place as Bill MacLeod, but is no relation. Tony's early days were spent "tossing cabers," throwing hammers and playing shinty in the championship class. If you don't know what the game of shinty is like as played in the north of Scotland, just think of all the rigorous sports you can, add them together, then multiply the rigours a few times and you have a faint idea of shinty.

Nothing would do the B.B.C. boys but that they must ride with Tony on the footplate during one of his regular trips (these Highlanders have, as I've already said, splendid speaking voices). So Tony, much against his wish, had a galaxy of young and eager lads on his engine; and, of course Tony gave them all they wanted, just by being himself. But he sighed with relief when it was all over, for he is one of the shyest of lads.

He didn't sigh with relief for long. His face was red the next morning, when a very good artist's impression of him appeared in a prominent paper and an enthusiastic reporter captioned it with "The Locospotters' Pin-up Driver," or some such nonsense. I can't recall the exact words of that caption, but Tony's comments on the "pin-up" bit are printed on my mind forever. Unfortunately, they're not for publication, but I can say that they carried the maximum amount of superheat.

To end this brief survey of a few of my generation who left their mark on the history of the East Coast "fasts" I feel that one other should be selected from the many at Haymarket who did so.

Jim Paterson, like Tony MacLeod, was big in every way. He drove No. 60009 regularly, and is possibly an outstanding example of an engineman who was intended for another, and quite different career. Jim studied to become a missionary and actually trained as such, and while he remained on the footplate, he also managed to combine his two vocations. He is well-known in Baptist circles in many parts of Britain as a lay preacher and writer in the columns of their publications.

He retired the year prior to my writing this, and right to the end of his driving career he held to the tradition of the school of drivers who taught him their ways. He possibly was out of his generation, but that in no way dimmed the quality of his real impact as an engineman. He resolutely refused to abuse his engine, if he thought that it was an unnecessary act, and was forthright in stating his reasons for not doing so if he was called in question—no matter who the questioner was. He put up some really good performances on the East Coast expresses, and was one of the most systematic drivers at Haymarket. He is the proud possessor of a watch he received for good work during those floods, which, as I've already mentioned, put the main line between Dunbar and Berwick out of action. He was on one of the Edinburgh-London trains going the alternative Waverley route when part of that road also became suddenly submerged. Jim was prompt to see the danger to trains coming the other way, and took suitable preventative action. He himself would not want his action to be "blown up," but I can say that what he did that day required other qualities as well as resource, and those same qualities were an inherent part of his character.

Jim's chief claim to inclusion in this book is his record for economy in running his engine. While never a "speed at any price" merchant, he nevertheless put up some very good high-speed performances in his day, but it was his consistency and ease of working an engine which characterised his whole driving career. Shortly before he retired I was speaking to an official who said of Jim Paterson: "I couldn't always see eye-to-eye with him in the discussions we've had on train driving, but I believe that if the coal consumption charts were still in being Jim would be at the head of the Haymarket list."

When he left the footplate he told me himself the wrench it was to say goodbye to "9" and I know that the driver who fell heir to her got an engine in nearly as good condition as the day she came new from Doncaster works some twenty years ago.

Speaking of falling heir to an engine brings me to the point where I should say, as a conclusion to this chapter, a brief word about those lads who are now doing the job. Obviously there isn't room for the lot, but a "typical two" from Haymarket will indicate that my generation doesn't need think that they are the only ones who could "do their stuff" on the top link trains between the capitals of England and Scotland.

Tommy Smith and Bill Nairn are my selection as two who are typical present-day representatives of the top express drivers at Haymarket. Tommy Smith made his mark a long time ago when on the spare, as long ago as the high-speed era of the 1938 "Coronation" train.

I suppose everyone knows that the "Coronation" regular timings have not yet been restored, although the "Talisman" is coming pretty near the "Coronation" schedule as I'm writing this. Also from all the signs and portents I wouldn't be at all surprised if by the time this book is published there will be a train booked to run between Edinburgh and London as fast, if not faster than the "Coronation"; (that is, it will do 393 miles in 360 minutes, with two stops, York and Newcastle on the down trip, and the up run in the same time (although there was only one stop at Newcastle on the up "Coronation"). The "Coronation's" average speed was in the region of 65½mph with nine coaches weighing 310 tons.

That was the kind of train on which Tommy Smith showed them how to do it during one week, when the regular driver fell ill, and Tommy as the senior spare man took over. So remember, that the performance which is given wasn't the running of a regular driver with a regular engine, which is a very big factor in good running. Tommy Smith on both up and down runs for that week was driving more than one of the specially-built-for-the-job engines; what was more, there was no chance on the "Coronation" to tell any fancy tales about performance.

Each of the engines were fitted with a speed recorder with charting mechanism which, on a long roll of paper, told everything regarding speed, acceleration, braking, and so on. At the end of the week's running the charts which Tommy produced caused a minor sensation. I knew the official whose duty it was to unlock the sealed door of the little compartment which housed the charts (or graphs if you prefer it) and he told me that if you laid each of these tell-tale lengths of paper one on top of the other, they looked like carbon copies—so exactly alike was each to the first which came from the recorder that week.

In spite of this near perfection of high-speed running, Tommy left his hallmark on those graphs. Remember what I said about running to plan. Well, every engineman worth his salt isn't just content to do what's asked off him. He can, and does do that something extra which is the criterion of the *engineman* rather than the *driver.*

In my talk with Tommy to get the inside story of that week's running, as usual I discussed his "plan" and it is typical of him that he not only explained the "why", but produced his own times to show how it was done.

"So far as I was concerned," he said, "I had listened to the talk about the tight schedule on the "Coronation," but never agreed with the opinion that it was a difficult train to run, with engines like 4490 *Empire of India,* which if I mind rightly was one of the engines I drove that week."

"Naturally, as a senior spare man liable to be called on for East Coast running I had 'weighed up' the "Coronation" schedule, and was convinced I could better the timings between Edinburgh and Newcastle, and still not put a foot wrong on any of the speed restrictions. That week gave me an opportunity of proving my theory. I had five minutes in hand on arrival at Newcastle each day, not because I just wanted to run that much early to prove a theory, but because I thought the time allowance for taking water at Newcastle was on the neat side, and I wanted the lads who relieved me to have a decent start to a really harder trip than my own part of the job."

"How was it mainly done, Tommy? What was the 'cut-off' most of the time?" I asked.

"Never far away from 15 per cent, and quite often even less than that, with the full regulator at every proper opportunity, of course—and by-the-way," he added casually, "here's my actual running times. I've copied them from my diary."

Here are his times:

	Schedule	Actual running
Waverley	4.30	
Drem	4.49	
Dunbar	5.58	½ minute early
Grantshouse	5.9½	½ minute early
Berwick	5.25	Time
Belford	5.37½	1 minute early
Alnmouth	5 .51	2 minutes early
Morpeth	6.6½	3½ minutes early
Newcastle	6.25	5 minutes early

So much for performance. Now for experiences out of the usual.

Bill Nairn is an ex-Scots Guardsman and if I add that he's got all an old soldier's sense of the ridiculous it gives a pretty good idea of what Bill is like. Like all the top link men Bill has gone through the mill, and his comments are not only terse but very telling. He did a lot of real firing to many of the well-known North Eastern drivers who ran the East Coast expresses from Haymarket.

For instance, Bill's comments on Tommy Roper, one of the real characters among the top link North Eastern men to whom he fired, was that "he broke more clay pipes than any driver I fired to" and he added a yarn which no one is expected to believe without a pinch of salt.

"You never saw Tommy without a clay pipe in his mouth, you know, and one day after the usual disaster to it took place, and the pipe was smashed, I asked him why he didn't get a wooden pipe. So he had one in reserve the next day, and as usual the clay fell and was broken, but Tom was happy. He filled the wooden pipe, stuck it in his mouth, and the next thing I knew was a yell and the brake was being applied (we were doing well over seventy at the time)."

" 'Nip off Bill,' Tommy yelled, 'and get my pipe!' Then he realised that the pipe would be lying two miles behind by the time I could do this, so he shoved up the brake handle and resigned himself to a smokeless trip. If I'd been as fond of a pipe as Tommy I would have anchored it to my coat with a wee bit string," said the ever-practical Bill.

Bill Nairn drove the last train (the Pullman) to get through before the bridges came down during the flooding I've already mentioned between Dunbar and Berwick, but he wasn't quite so lucky when he returned from Newcastle via the Waverley route. At Tynehead, the floods caught up with him, and he stood with his train from 8pm the one day until 10am the next. To hear Bill's account of that experience kept me grinning, but there was a lot more behind it than the laughs, even with the picture of big Bill and his fireman standing in the cab of 60519 with nothing on but their boots, and the cab festooned with "washing hanging out to dry." Luckily it was August, but it couldn't have been nice wading waist-deep in muddy flowing water to the signalbox in an attempt to bring assistance to the stranded passengers in that train.

Assistance *did* arrive in the shape of motor buses to take the folk home by road, but by this time a goat which was in the guard's van was "out for the count" for lack of sustenance, while a few of the humans weren't in much better shape. Consultation between the guard and Bill resulted in the latter dragging the goat to one of the buses—where it was deposited on the back seat apparently unconscious.

Bill, the guard, and the fireman meanwhile buckled to in assisting the passengers to leave the train and board the buses, and were more than busy on the job. But when they were able to relax at last, Bill thought it was high time to give that goat some treatment, so he gathered all the vegetation he could off the higher ground, and made for the bus, where "Billy" was supposed to be lying in dire straits.

"But I needn't have bothered," grinned Bill. "By the time I got there, the darned animal had wakened up, eaten most of the back seat, and was starting on the bodywork of the coach, until I distracted its attention with more tasty nourishment."

Bill started driving in 1924, and has done plenty since that date. He was the driver who took Winston Churchill on one of the stages of his journey during the last war, when the Prime Minister was on his way to meet Roosevelt "somewhere in the Atlantic." The result of that meeting was seen shortly afterwards when America entered the war on the side of the Allies. The German airmen were after that train with bombs and flares. "At Acklington it was like daylight with the flares dropping all round" was Bill's only comment on a trip which will stand out in history for more reasons than one.

Unusual experiences seem to have come Bill's way all along the path of his career. In 1947, the year of the big blizzards, the East Coast trains were sometimes taking two days to force a passage from Edinburgh to London. The drivers never knew just when they would get back once they started off.

On one of these occasions Bill and his mate had had a very tough trip making Newcastle—so long, in fact, did it take that they were instructed to travel home as passengers with the first train which managed to get through from the south. Like the old campaigner he is, Bill loaded up with provisions which he bought at Newcastle before joining the train. "It's a good job too, for we got stuck here and there for hours, and the solitary lady who was in our compartment was mighty glad of the sandwiches we offered," he told me. Then, the ice broken, she told Bill and his mate the story.

It appears she was returning from London, where she had been to Buckingham Palace to receive an honour of some kind for her smart work in spotting a German spy during the war. The spy was dressed as a nun, but he was given away by his hands, which were obviously a man's to the shrewd observant eyes of the lady sitting opposite him in an English train. Bill thinks the lady in question was a teacher from Alnwick.

Bill Nairn has still a good few years in which to add to his collection of unusual experiences. But they are the frills which adorn the job he does on the footplate of *William Whitelaw,* and his doings make a strong finish to a brief survey of a few of the "speed merchants" who handle the Gresleys on the road where their capabilities have never yet been stretched to the limit of their capacity.

In a book such as this I think it is not only permissible but long overdue that the curtain should be raised a little on what happens before the act begins, to pay tribute to the fellows whom the spotlight never seems to hit. As one of the actors, so to speak, I've always been very conscious of the debt I owe to the back stage galaxy of real talent which saw to it that *Spearmint* and others of the Gresley breed were there to join in the play.

At Haymarket we had a bunch of running foremen who were second to none, and it is of them and the locomotive inspectors I would like to tell you.

XII

The Badge of the Bowler Hat

While it is true that nowadays you see a motive power supervisor or inspector under a bowler hat, the cult of this distinctive headgear is dying out among the "N.C.O's" in the locomotive fraternity.

Like most of the traditional practices in locomotive history the "bowler" had reasons for its adoption apart from its utility purpose. As an indication to the lowly that here was a superior it had its effect. (I can vouch for that through experience). When to the hat was added a beard, and a solemn, almost pontifical manner of address and bearing, the effect on the simple mind was impressive. In my very young days I used to go into a fit of stammers at the very thought of having to justify either my actions or even my existence to such a being. So I kept remote from them, and coloured their real character from my own misguided imagination. Of course, my early assessment couldn't have been more wrong, and maybe that's one of the reasons why I want to pay tribute to their grade in this book—that and the fact that I do not think they receive anything like the credit they deserve as back-room boys of the highest merit.

In selecting Ross Dougan of Haymarket as a representative of the Running Foremen (we still call them supervisors unofficially) I'm doing so because I believe that he is typical of what his breed should be. On the job Ross is more regimental than a regimental sergeant-major. He would report his own grandfather if he stepped out of the line of locomotive rectitude or break the code which had been laid down. "Off the string," however, he's a good sociable type, and possibly the day after reporting you, he will present you with a large bunch of his prize roses with a careless abandon which says "there's plenty more where those come from." The background of experience behind "Doug" is really phenomenal and as few supervisors normally reach the top link before promotion to the bowler comes their way it's in their firing and early driving days that the interest lies.

"Doug" isn't a "native-born" Haymarket man. He started in St. Margarets, when that depot worked a lot more of the glamorous passenger trains than it does today. "Doug" as a fireman was the most frequently selected in his day to work Royal Trains and other "plum" trips which fell to the superefficient engineman away back in 1922. This was when such work was given to specially selected engine crews, and not, as is today's usual practice in many depots to the crew on the top link nearest the turn of duty when a Royal or other V.I.P. train is to be run.

In 1922 Ross Dougan was the fireman on the engine of the train which carried King George V and Queen Mary on their way to the north of Scotland, and again fired the engine which had as passengers the Duke and Duchess of York (later King George VI and Queen Elizabeth) on their way to Cupar to open the war memorial there.

Ross Dougan, stocky and strong as an ox, just could not be broken on any tough firing spot, and reckons that the toughest day's goods firing he ever encountered in a tough career was on an 18 inch cylinder N.B. 0-6-0, one of the Matthew Holmes type. This day the tender was coaled sky-high at St. Margarets (Edinburgh) and a full load was taken from Edinburgh goods yard to Carlisle (99 miles).

That may not look so impressive nowadays with the high capacity goods engines we have, but those old "eighteen inchers" could "worry" the coal to some tune, and on this trip the tender was nearly stripped before the half-way mark at Hawick, where "Doug" had to clean the fire and "coal" the tender for the second lap.

As a regular fireman on the top link goods at St. Margarets he worked the Edinburgh to Aberdeen goods with engine 851, a Reid 0-6-0 of N.B. Class "B" (now "J35"). On that job he had to clean the fire half-way on the 131 miles' trip, and then shovel the coal forward for the return run before "booking off."

"What is the toughest passenger trip on which you've fired, Doug?" I asked him, when he, Bill Nairn, and myself, were yarning one night.

"That day on 'Scott' No. 423 *Quentin Durward,*" he replied, "when we did 386 miles with a passenger special from Edinburgh to Hawick, then from Hawick to Aberdeen, and from Aberdeen back to Edinburgh for one day's work—and nary a bean in the way of mileage payment," he added, looking at Bill who works mileage turns as a top link man.

As a driver Ross Dougan was the first "spare" Haymarket man to work the "Coronation," possibly because he knew the Edinburgh to Newcastle road better than most of us at that time, having fired on the "Newcastle beer" a train which traverses the little-known Border Counties section of the old N.B. This train had quite a reputation in the early days for speed and difficulty in working, between Duddingston (a few miles out of Edinburgh) and Newcastle.

But then young "Doug" had as a regular driver a legendary figure in the annals of North British railway history. He fired for years to "Sandy" Lawrie, who had the reputation of knowing every road in the North British system. Sandy and "Doug" along with *Quentin Durward* could be met in the furthest reaches of the West Highland; they could be seen streaking to Carlisle, Aberdeen, Perth, and any other of the places which were in these days almost sacrosanct to other depots, engines and men.

Sandy's memory for roads was so phenomenal that he could sit down in the "bothy" at St. Margarets and detail meticulously, to a foot, the position of any signal, bridge, platform, or any other landmark on the N.B. system. To appreciate thoroughly what this means it should be realised that in the old days each depot within a railway company had its well defined "area of operation" beyond which the enginemen seldom ran without a conductor.

Between them Sandy and Ross made *Quentin Durward* legendary, too. As an engineman "Sandy" was "good plus," to put it mildly. All the years he drove 423 it went from one shops overhaul to the next without even a big-end brass needing attention. As for Ross, he almost rubbed that engine out of existence; on the dullest day it looked like a sunburst—you could hardly look at it for the dazzle.

This, then, is the lad who came to Haymarket as a driver in 1925. Had he not done so he would have lost two shillings a day, due to the period of redundancy which put so many drivers and firemen down the promotional ladder. Naturally that sort of thing caused someone to be pushed back a little, and the fellow whom Ross displaced in the seniority list was Bill Nairn.

"In spite of that," said Ross, "Bill gave me all the little tips and hints which are so helpful to a newcomer, and we became the best of pals." "Yes, that's right, but it didn't prevent him reporting me, the only time in my life I was late" growled Bill. Which goes to show, as I've already said, the type of bloke who makes a good running foreman.

If I had a slogan to compile about the duties of a motive power running foreman I'd borrow that one so often plugged in stories and scenes in the theatre and cinema—"the show must go on." How the show does go on is only known to those in it. The running foreman doesn't even get one round of applause.

Among a hundred other duties it is the running foreman's job to see that the engines leave the depot on time, and while this normally isn't so very difficult at a shed like Haymarket, now and again a hefty spanner gets thrown into the works (very often nearly literally). Then it is that a good supervisor is proven, and like a good driver you only know how good he is when he runs into difficulties. I was once involved, and had the opportunity of seeing Ross Dougan during one of these proving periods. Strangely enough it was the engine which Bill Nairn now drives which was the centre of the trouble and the trouble arose because of the geography of a part of Haymarket depot.

Gresley Pacific *William Whitelaw* was being prepared to run the 10.50am Edinburgh-London that morning. The driver who was preparing her decided there wasn't enough coal on the tender so he made for the coal shed. (That was before Haymarket had a coal hopper as it has today). At that time of the morning the normal road into the coal shed was jammed with a queue of engines slowly moving under the two stages where hutches of coal could be tipped on to their tenders. To take up position behind that long line was going to waste a lot of time, and there's no time to be wasted by a preparing man with a string of engines to get ready "on the dot." So this lad had a bright idea; he would use another road which led into the centre of the queue, hold up the rear engines, and slip into position in the coal road; thus he would get *William* coaled more quickly and save time.

Unfortunately, this bypass road on which he stood cut across the road up which the coal wagons were propelled on a steep incline to the coal shed. And there was *William Whitelaw* standing foul of this incline when the shunting pilot pushed the coal a little further into the shed. At least that's what the driver thought he was going to do, until he got an outsize bump from the battery end, and that immense weight of coal started to push him relentlessly down the incline right amidships into the dignified *William*.

Gently but firmly that "pug" lifted the trailing end of the engine and the leading tender end of that Gresley, and deposited them on the sleepers. I was standing by with another engine waiting for coal, and I'll swear there was a look of pained surprise about *William* as it lay "all awry." "Doug" was on duty that morning, and I fully expected him to order another engine for the job. But I did not know "Doug." That was the regular engine, and come "hell or high water" it was going on the "ten-fifty."

How he organised things so quickly I've yet to ask him, but in no time at all there was a swarm of fitters, drivers, firemen, and others round the pained *William,* ministering to its needs. They prepared it on the spot. They brought re-railing ramps and battens of wood and this and that for the first-aid treatment of the bruised "A4." Fitters were loosening bits and pieces, and "packing up" the vital points, so that when the "ambulance," in the shape of the breakdown crane, arrived from St. Margarets, all they had to do was lower the jib, fix the hooks, and lift the helpless *William* on to its feet again. A slick move into the coal shed, and a final mechanical examination on the pit by the fitter followed, and just as the train driver "signed on," *William Whitelaw,* his own engine, was standing at the shed signal waiting for the road.

That bald description perhaps conveys little, but you can take my word for it (and any engineman will verify what I say) that it was a really good performance organised by a director who not only was letter-perfect in the play, but knew his cast outside in, and knew how to use them to the best advantage.

Nowadays I travel in first class carriages, and occasionally listen to intellectual discourses from profound gentlemen who appear to know how to run our railways better than railwaymen. I listen to their cracks, and now and again take the trouble to go into details to give "cause and effect" of something which earns their criticisms of "darned inefficiency." Quite often I don't bother to contradict them. I just sit looking at them and think.

I think of that morning when Glasgow was being blitzed by the German planes which were streaming across Haymarket on their way to destroy. I think about Ross Dougan going from engine to engine as we were getting them ready, almost by "feel." I see him here-there-and-everywhere, assisting us all he could—dashing for oil for this man; helping with the sand pails on another fellow's engine; and ducking beneath the "guts" of another to oil the shaft—until at the finish of his shift, he scribbled on his daily report "All engines left to time."

Maybe we deserve the criticisms which come thick and fast in the columns of the press and the compartments of first and second class coaches. Maybe as a biased onlooker, I should not even venture to excuse by explaining; but biased or not there's one thing I can say with truth—so long as the railway N.C.O's are of the stamp of "Doug" (and there's a lot of them) the criticisms won't worry me very much.

Jock Todd is an inspector to whom I've often said "you're a good driver wasted." He was not only a good driver, but along with Jim Swan, Jock Bartholomew, and myself formed what might be called the hard core of the Mutual Improvement Class at Haymarket when it came to birth, and for many years after.

Jock is as big as a house, with legs about as thick as my waist, and at one time you would normally find him during his off moments trying to get lost in the Cairngorm mountains, or hanging by his eyebrows from snow cornices on Ben Nevis, or diving off Granton pier as the clock was striking midnight on "Auld Years' Nicht." He delighted in east winds, and if it hadn't been for convention I'm sure he wouldn't even have worn dungarees. As it was, there was little or nothing under the dungarees, summer or winter. Even to think of him used to make the goose pimples come out all over me. He was caricatured once by an artist, who showed Jock standing drying himself at the seaside, with an urchin enquiring "Excuse me, sir, is this your icicle?" The scene, of course, was laid deep in snow.

He's so "scientific" that when he used to give us lectures in the class room I had to implore him before he started: "For heaven's sake speak plain English to the boys, and don't forget you're speaking to *them,* not to the formulae or circles and angles you're so fond of scribbling on the blackboard."

You can't (even nowadays) keep him out of a kilt, and in spite of the fact that there's not a drop of Highland blood in his veins he speaks Gaelic. Not content with that, he holidays on the coast of France and if rumours are correct he's now engaged in teaching the natives how to speak their own idiom. In spite of all these " defects " Jock Todd is a real dyed-in-the-wool engine-man, otherwise he wouldn't have left his cushy office job, where he worked as a youngster for a pittance, and come for an equally small pittance to learn the locomotive game. He could quite as easily have entered a drawing office, for he is a first class draughtsman, or the technical side of engineering, but he wanted to get on to the footplate like all his engine-daft buddies; and I know they had to wrench him *off* the footplate almost by main force to make him an inspector. It says on the inspectorial pass he carries: "The holder is authorised to advise and-instruct ... " or words to that effect; and I know no man with better capabilities for so doing.

Jock makes model engines, and if the need arose could dismantle and assemble *Spearmint* with the greatest of aplomb. With all this talent in him, it wasn't surprising that surprising things were done on the engines he fired (not always to the peace of mind of his drivers in the early days).

He nearly frightened one of his drivers out of his wits one day, by calmly taking off the cover on the Westinghouse equalising valve, placing a thick piece of plate glass where the cover should be, and working the brake application handle, just to verify for himself the action of that large circular valve. That he was working with pressures of 75 and 90lb. to the square inch didn't trouble Jock at all. Jock was, and still is, a seeker after truth, and the fact that he often got it proved more than once a little embarrassing to folk who should have known the answers. Also it proved of great benefit to the lads who came to hear him expound his views in the classrooms where we met regularly.

Naturally enough he was the star fireman of his day at Haymarket and from the moment his name proudly headed the roster marked "Spare Express Passenger Fireman" he started to go places, and one of the places he went one morning was the platform at Haymarket station to fire on one of the Edinburgh-Aberdeen trains to driver Tom Henderson. Of Tom Henderson, and *Hazeldean,* his N.B. Atlantic, I have written before, but I think a brief repeat reference here won't prove out of place. Tom always reminded me of the pictures you see of the Vikings. Huge and lithe, with breadth where it was needed, high cheek-boned with fierce eyes, a hook nose and long moustache, he and *Hazeldean* went roaring on the Aberdeens, the pair of them battling for the mastery. He named his house after that engine. To fire to Tom was considered an adventure for a spare fireman, and young Jock Todd wasn't quite sure of his reception when he appeared for Tom's regular mate, who had suddenly taken ill. Tom merely looked at Jock from head to foot, grunted, and stepped into the cab when the train arrived at Haymarket.

"I knew the drill for Tom," said Jock to me. "Tom had no fancy ideas about where the steam pressure should be—it should be blowing heavens hard from the safety valves. Tom had no time for any fireman who couldn't keep it that way, so I acted accordingly."

"Like yourself, I liked the look of the N.B. Atlantic, but they swung a bit and burned a lot of coal"—at which mild understatement from the meticulous Jock I raised my eyebrows.

"Oh yes, I know what you think of them," he grinned, "and I agree they took you for a ride all right. That first experience with Henderson still sticks in my mind. Passing Muchalls the cab executed a half-circle from one side to the other. I looked over to Tom. He was sitting quite serene with his arm round the reversing lever, so I said to myself this must be the usual performance, I had better get used to it."

Jock later fired to Tom, and his "He was a grand driver" was a real tribute to Henderson.

"I found that if you were willing to work and do your job properly you could get on well with Henderson as I did, and he was a great worker himself. I missed him that first day at Kirkcaldy, and found him on the bogie with half-a-bale of cotton-waste cleaning down the smokebox. Like all the old drivers he took an immense pride in his engine, which, if I remember correctly, caused Jock Bartholomew to write another verse.

"Down through Fordoun she could *run,*
With a shine on the smokebox like the rising sun,
With Tom at the lever, and Jock in the hold,
You can tell who you like, she did look bold.

And bold they must have been, for it is on record among the Haymarket men of Tom's generation, that the stationmaster at Fordoun, watching Tom's progress, used to say to the signalman: "Thank God they're past." He needn't have worried—it may have looked terrific but there was no more knowledgeable driver on the ways of the N.B. Atlantic than Tom Henderson. He was heard to declare once: "They won't coup—I've tried it." This was Tom's way of saying he knew their limits and wouldn't go beyond the danger mark.

At that time Tom was driving 876 *Waverly.* It was later that he had 878 *Hazeldean,* on which Jock fired to him during a memorable test, and as I do not think the real story of that test has been told, Jock can shed an interesting light on a bit of locomotive history which has been the subject of controversy since it took place over three decades ago.

After the grouping of the old railway companies Tom Henderson and Jock Todd took part in this test between a North Eastern, a Great Northern, and a North British Atlantic. Tom's engine was *Hazeldean* and Jock thinks that this was the first N.B. engine to be fitted with a steam chest pressure gauge.

As could be expected the North Eastern Atlantic returned by far the lowest figures for coal consumption. In the first place she was driven by Harry Potts of Gateshead (later Inspector Potts). Secondly, Harry was not only as "good as they make 'em, but had the advantage of being on his home ground and knew every inch of the road. Any engineman will tell you just how big an advantage that can be. Thirdly, from my own experience of driving N.E. Atlantics I know that there wasn't an engine of her class which burned less coal during her normal day-to-day running. Using specially selected engines—with which, I take it, all such tests are run—it was a foregone conclusion, but a week's running with all the engines and crews based on Newcastle, proved the superiority of the N.E. Atlantic beyond doubt.

At the conclusion of the test, however, the officials were convinced that the coal consumption figures of the N.B. Atlantics were a good deal higher than they ought to be, so a further trial was ordered, and this time Tom Henderson was instructed where to put the reversing lever so that *Hazeldean* would run with a shorter cut-off. Jock was told to stop the blowing off at the safety valves, and off they set.

Tom pulled *Hazeldean* up to the sixth notch as he had been instructed, but the engineman in him could only stand that for so long. The driving boxes started to knock, and that was too much for Tom. "Coal consumption or no coal consumption" he said to Jock, as he let the lever forward into the fourth notch, "I'm ruining my engine for no bunch of folk in any so-and-so test."

And that was that. He absolutely refused to run his engine except where he wanted, in justice to that engine and to the peace of his own mind.

"I think he was quite right" said Jock, "for I am convinced that the N.B. piston valve engines were not designed for working with an early cut-off". (Incidentally, they fitted *Hazeldean* with a recording pyrometer outside the smokebox, and I was interested in the readings it gave.)

"With the long cut-off and low steam pressure in the steam-chest the steam passed through the superheater rapidly, and we never had a comparatively high superheat temperature. The dynamometer car fellows were very interested in the N.B. Atlantic with its inside admission piston valves, the N.E. Atlantics, as you know, having outside admission valves".

Tom Henderson wasn't very happy during those trials, and this was made evident when, after they were all over, and they were returning to Scotland, he roared to Jock; "Get these valves blowing, mate, there's no 'pounds to the mile' this time".

In 1928 Jock was sent to learn the road to York preparatory to working the first non-stop run between Edinburgh and London as fireman to Tom Henderson. Due to a shift back in the roster Jock missed that history making trip on the "Flying Scotsman", his place being taken by Bob McKenzie—now a supervisor at Keith. Jock, however, made the trip the following week with Tommy Roper, "the pipe breaker" I've already mentioned.

As a driver Jock managed to reach the regular runs on the Glasgow expresses before they pulled him off the footplate to act as firing instructor to the younger generation, while in between he travels on the engines as third man "to advise and instruct" when the occasion demands. He neither wears nor desires to wear a bowler hat as a badge of authority or impressiveness. Under the battered old trilby he affects there's loads and loads of stuff which is far more impressive than all the outward signs in the world, and I rather envy these lads who have the benefit of his instruction when he talks to them about firing a railway engine.

In his day he could guarantee to see every signal on the road he fired (and this is a matter not only of pride, but of duty, with him). He was the slickest manipulator of a firing shovel at Haymarket, where there are few sloths at the game. He consistently fired his engines so that he caught sight of the "distant" signal, whipped in "a round of the box" and was ready to see the "home" signal and all the others in the section. The safety rule which says "a fireman when not otherwise engaged must keep a good look-out" was no empty form of words to Jock Todd.

Jock's system, his whole approach to the job, is typical of the best which is in the locomotive inspectorial grades on the railways of today, and while their experience has mostly been with a unit of power which is due to become obsolete, this does not alter the principle of their mental approach. It is this rather than their "instruction and advice" which is the valuable factor in the work they are performing.

XIII
Mainly North Eastern

Before I drove the regular East Coast expresses with my own Gresley "A3", I had run the Edinburgh-Newcastle road so often that I got to know it almost better than my own native North British area. For several years on the senior spare, I sampled most of the engines which the N.E.R. commonly used at that time, on such trains as the "Flying Scotsman", the "Aberdonian" and the "Night Scotsman."

That is, I handled the three-cylinder Atlantics—the "Zs", the two cylinder "Vs", the "Booster," and very infrequently an "R" 4-4-0. With the latter I was unfortunate and I knew it. During the few times I drove the "Rs," I never once got free steam, but I'm willing to believe what my North Eastern colleagues told me about them, for they should know them well enough.

Alex ("Sandy") Davidson (whom legend said had driven more express mileage than any other driver in Britain), was one of the original North Eastern men at Haymarket who did nothing else as a fireman or a driver except East Coast express work. "Sandy" assured me that in his day the Class "Rs" ran express trains regularly and were wonderful engines. When I drove them they were on the way to the scrap heap, but even then I could sense their comfortable riding qualities at high speed, and more particularly I could nearly tolerate the right-hand drive, when it was possible to look over the boiler and see the left hand side of the track—at least a good deal better than I could on the Atlantics.

The North Eastern certainly knew what to do in designing a locomotive for high speed when they put the "Z" on the road. I drove many of them, and even when they were in the "sere and yellow" they never lost that feeling of "breed" which one expects in a really fast locomotive. The same couldn't be said about the "V," which not only rolled when they were a bit decrepit, but burned about twice the amount of coal the "Z" did.

Naturally I did not, and never will, like any engine which has the controls so positioned that the driver sits on the right-hand side. I've argued this with many of the men brought up on this way of driving, and quite often have been told "But on our road the signals are positioned for seeing from the right hand side."

By nature I'm a polite chap, and this prevented me from saying "Baloney to that, mate," for the fact of the matter is that on most of the old companies, the reason for the "right-hand drive" had its roots in the days when signalling wasn't what it is nowadays, and drivers had to watch the opposite line and give passing enginemen the "tip-off." In fact the old N.E. gauge lamp had red, green, and white glasses, which served the dual purpose of showing the boiler water level, or being used for signalling. Those same gauge lamps were part of the engine kit which I drew for 2193, 2194, or 714, which were the N.E. "Zs" at Haymarket.

Again, on the old engines, like the N.E. "R" for instance, the driver's line of vision was not obstructed to the same extent as later occurred when the Atlantics made their appearance with a long and high boiler. All the N.B. engines were left-hand drive, and while I got used through time to sitting on the right-hand side of more than the N.E. types, I was never completely happy for one reason and one only.

All my driving career I have subjected myself to a rigid and quite uncompromising mental attitude to the safety factor in locomotive operation, and one of the main factors in the safety code to me was an unimpeded view (as far as possible) between the driver and any measures which might be taken to attract his attention during an emergency.

That is my objection to "right-hand drive" engines briefly outlined, but perhaps it could be better understood if a practical illustration is given of the sort of thing I have in mind. While I am not identifying the place for obvious reasons, the incident quoted is not only one of quite a few which took place during my normal running of express trains, but is indicative of an engineman's interpretation of the safety code.

It was a pitch dark, windy night, or rather early morning. I was working the down "Aberdonian" from Newcastle to Edinburgh with a right-hand drive engine. On the up run we had passed Goswick loop, where a train was lying a mangled mass of twisted wreckage—they were still taking out the dead as we inched our train past the tragic spot.

As we cleared the "slow" and I was "notching her up" my mate put a question to me: "How long have you been driving express trains?"

I made a rough guess.

"Can you honestly say," he continued, "that during all those years you have never taken a chance with a signal when you couldn't see it, or it was a doubtful one?"

"Nary a chance," I said.

"What did you do?"

"Put the brake on pronto," I said.

That finished the conversation. We were both too busy after that, but coming back on the "Aberdonian" some four hours later I recalled that conversation.

We would be doing 80 when it happened. From my right-hand seat I should have caught a green flash from the distant in the inward curve of the smoke-box where it joins the saddle on the framing. A few seconds later the curve of the road should have brought the signal light into full view from the left-hand side, and normally my mate would have given me a hand signal to verify that flash I had seen.

But for some reason my mate was busy (the high wind was responsible for that) and at the spot where I should have got a glimpse of the signal from my seat on the right-hand side I saw nothing, neither yellow nor green. I stepped across the cab just in time to see it. The signal (a colour light) was out.

I stretched out my hand (not even taking the time to cross the cab again) and pulled the brake handle to zero. We stopped all right, on the proper side of the home signal showing red, and in the darkness ahead I could see the faint glimmer of the level crossing gates and the dim shape of a vehicle crossing the line.

"That," I said to my mate, "is what you do when a distant signal can't be seen or is doubtful."

While that cannot be classed as an "emergency proper," just think what actually happens when one does arise. Assume, for instance, that you see a piled-up train blocking both lines and you are not only a non-railwayman, but that you don't even have the sketchiest idea of what a railwayman would do in an emergency.

Even the dimmest layman would realise that danger threatened an on-coming train, and would do something to attract the driver's attention. And if he did attempt that, he certainly wouldn't stand between the up and down lines—as naturally as a stream runs down a hill he would make for the left-hand side of the track and do his "dashing hero" stuff to the best of his knowledge and ability.

Under normal conditions, this or that awkwardness doesn't much matter, but as a driver of high-speed trains over many years, I've insisted on "catering for the abnormal" in every aspect of safety and you can take my word for it that it has paid dividends more than once. Now that I've justified my rudeness to the man who tries to tell me that his road is signalled for right-hand driving I'd like to say a brief word about the right-hand drive N.E. Atlantics and how we got on together.

When you drove a "Z" or a "V" you had to adopt the crouching attitude of a jockey at the most tense moment of a classical race. This may look all right as an indication to the outside viewer that you're "streamlined for speed," but quite honestly it's not at all necessary on a railway engine. I like to sit as comfortably relaxed as possible, and couldn't care less for making an impression.

The seat on the N.E. Atlantic was broad enough almost to serve as a bed; your feet rested comfortably on a built-up footstool, and in this respect they were the acme of comfort, that is, if you could sit properly and catch your signals through the front cab window.

But when you passed through the first tunnel and the front window became obscured by blobs of sooty muck there was nothing else for it but to crouch on your seat like a half-shut jack-knife, and stick your head out at the side in the approved style supposed to be that adopted by high-speed enginemen (at least I've seen quite a few pictures where this seems to be the common idea).

The reason for the "crouch" on the "Z" was the *height* of the driving seat. It was on a level with the bottom of the side window, and even my meagre torso and head combined measure more than the length between the top and bottom of a cab side window.

In this position your eyes had no protection, and for this reason I carried goggles which I constantly used on the N.B. and N.E. Atlantics, especially at night, for even if the front windows did not get obscured, the reflected glare from the firebox showed you a beautiful picture of yourself; but this is poor compensation even to the vainest, if it prevents you seeing the signals. Curiously enough the wearing of goggles to protect the eyes from cinders (of which there were more than enough, especially on the N.B. Atlantics) was not a widespread custom among my mates in the days of which I write. In fact, goggles were rather frowned on by officialdom for some reason.

On the top of the driving seat of the "Z" two apertures were cut, while at the side was the long slot where the reversing lever pointer worked. This slot had a brass plate calibrated with numbers, but not percentage cut-offs as is now indicated on modern engines. The two apertures on the top of the seat were to allow access to two short handles, which when turned through an angle of about fifty degrees actuated the steam reversing gear. One handle gave the gear direction, i.e., "back or forward," the other admitted steam to the flat valve which actuated the gear. At least, you hoped it would.

This steam reverser was always a source of profound speculation to me when I drove the N.E. Atlantics. It must be remembered that a "spare" driver has a relatively more difficult time of it than the driver of a regular engine. The spare man possibly handles as many as a dozen different engines on as many trains during a week's working, and of course has no chance of knowing the little idiosyncrasies of each engine he is asked to drive.

So there I would sit on the driving seat, shove up the "ram's-horn" throttle handle and glide away with a duplicate of one of the night expresses to London ("glide" is the only way to describe the beautiful motion of a "Z") The only thing on my mind was the question "How's the darned thing going to behave on this one?" The "thing," of course, was the steam reverser.

Fortunately the start out of Waverley station was easy and after one harrowing experience when the reversing lever jumped into full back gear with the throttle open, I used this easy start downhill to notch the engine up. If you were watching the N.E. Atlantics I drove, you would have seen a brief gap between the even exhausts coming from the chimney top. That was when I shut the throttle completely before going into the routine of shortening the valve cut-off. I always did this rather than risk a second jump into back gear with an engine running forward, for those night trains carried sleeping passengers and it couldn't have been a comfortable experience lying in bed and having an engine jigging rock'n'roll fashion on the head of the train. I've experienced this, and I didn't like it, even for a brief period.

So with the throttle shut and the reversing handle in "back" the trick was to match your delicacy of touch as you worked the steam handle and the lever started to move back towards "centre." Sometimes it moved so sedately that there was no trouble in shutting off the steam and stopping the backward movement of the lever at the desired spot. On the other hand, no sooner did you let the merest whiff of steam touch the reversing valve than that pointer literally *sprang* backwards, and only the speed of lightning in shutting off the steam stopped its mad impulse to reach the other end of that slot.

Once the thing was stopped at "2½" (the point I found most suitable) you shoved a piece of broken spring into the slot to prevent the lever working forward, for never once can I recall the N.E. reverser being held in position by steam power alone. I believe this was due to a fundamental fault inherent in all flat valves once wear starts to take place, namely, steam passes the face; while this may not mean much bother elsewhere, on a steam reverser it meant the difference between "staying put" and edging forward once the reversing gear was subjected to the thrust of the working valves in the fore-end.

Once the "notching-up" business was firmly accomplished, both my mate and myself started to enjoy ourselves thoroughly, for the "Z" was one of the loveliest riding engines I have ever handled. She was beautifully set on the springs, and to feel her under you riding over crossings and round curves, where an N.B. Atlantic would have pitched and swung like a mad bull, was to realise that in engines as well as horses "breed" could be evidenced in their motion.

If the train was a light one (350 tons was the capacity load of the "Z" between Edinburgh and Newcastle and normally the duplicate trains I worked were somewhere in the region of 200 tons), I would possibly manage to wangle the train up the 1 in 90 to Grantshouse without having to alter the valve cutoff, for quite frankly I hated the thought of working that steam reverser when the throttle was wide open on a bank.

Incidentally, that was the reason why I set the lever at "2½". On the easy stretches a "Z" could do her stuff with a full load in "2" or even "1½" from centre gear, but on a bank like Cockburnspath it had to be a very light train for the "Z" to take it in "2½" even. With a full load I soon learned that nothing less than full fore gear would surmount the obstacle presented by a seven-mile gradient of mostly 1 in 90, so I had a drill for this.

Just before the final rise there was a slight dip, and as we gained speed through this I shut the throttle, eased back the reverser to allow me to extract the plate, and allowed the gear to slide forward at its own sweet will into "full forward." The "Z" was the only engine I ever handled which could stand this treatment of a full throttle opening with the valves working full travel for miles, and still steam, to say nothing of one injector keeping up the boiler level without apparent difficulty.

On the five-mile downward stretch between Grantshouse and Reston the road is the very antithesis of the formula for a straight line. It winds in voluptuous curves which at high speed weren't too comfortable on any other type of engine (until the Gresley Pacific came along), but with the "Zs" I used to experiment for the sheer joy of watching their way on these curves. I have repeatedly run that five miles in four minutes, with the "Z" cuddling the curves like a sinuous snake round a particularly smooth tree. Not a quiver or harsh movement broke the spell of that performance, even when the engines were in a bad way mechanically, and I drove them when they were in that decrepit state eventually.

It was the same faultless speed performance on my favourite "racing" stretch on this grand railroad. This was on the return trip from Newcastle where, after we had mounted the five-mile climb between Alnmouth and Little Mill, ahead of us lay something like fifteen miles of high speed running, first down a moderate bank, then on to a very gentle downward (almost level) "prize length" of track which couldn't have been more ideally suited for a "Z" to show off.

On the first gradient I could feel the "Z" snuggling down to enjoy herself, purring at the chimney top, and as the speed rose to what would be considered a top crescendo, I almost closed the regulator until there was no sound at all from the light exhaust. I could almost believe there were no rails at all between the "blips" of the driving wheels over the joints. Then would come that final three miles of "prize length". Without the slightest further encouragement from the throttle the "Z" just flattened out and devoured these miles in one prolonged gurgling swallow. That, of course, is sheer imaginative nonsense, but it conveys my impression of this engine much better than if I drooled out the usual superlatives like "rocketing, terrific speed" and so on, and adding to this the percentage cut-off and regulator positions.

To me the "Z" had many points of criticism. They were difficult to prepare and stable, and the valve glands seemed incapable of remaining steam tight, due to the "outside admission" of the steam, but if I had an epitaph to write of them I think I'd say they were not only built for speed, but *enjoyed* that for which they were designed. Old engines, like old drivers, had their faults, but these can be forgotten in the charity which decency extends to the departed, and so far as I am concerned they departed from my ken many years ago.

Haymarket had visits from quite a few of the North Eastern "experiments." The "oil burner" came there regularly in the hands of Gateshead men, while the "Uniflow" engine, with its curious sharp blast like a motor car, was one of the regulars. I drove this engine once or twice and thought highly of its performance.

There was a yarn current at the time which showed how nicknames stick.

"How is the 'Uniflow' doing," a schoolboy asked the driver one day at the Waverley.

"The Uniflow? Never heard of it" says the driver. "That's it you're driving," says the scientific young one.

"That's not the Uniflow, son, that's 'stumpy'," says the driver. And he was quite right, for Herr Stumpf's engine got no other name amongst North Eastern enginemen.

Then there was that over-prolonged experiment called the "booster." I drove this engine also, and believe that if they could have invented a steam-tight flexible pipe joint this idea would have been a grand one on the hills of the N.B. railway. It was a curious feeling to ride on this engine, say up Cocksburnpath, and as the speed petered out on the gradient, suddenly feel as if a pilot had slipped behind you to jockey you up the hill; then, when a certain speed was attained, the "pilot" disappeared, as it were. As I have said, however, the steam pipes to the "booster" were a real source of annoyance, and every time I drove them with the booster working, I sat in a fog from the pipe joints which were never, as far as I experienced, steam tight.

Those years with the North Eastern engines and men I count the most rewarding of my driving career, and while it may seem as if my criticism of the things I personally did not like does not appear to bear this out, I would like it understood that there was much I admired in the N.E. set-up.

There was Gateshead shed, for instance. We had nothing like this on the North British.

It forms one side of a rough square, with the, King Edward and High Level bridges forming two sides, and Newcastle station making the opposite side of the square to Gateshead Shed. Trains can enter Newcastle station from any direction, engines can uncouple from their trains and go into the shed, and return to the station without ever needing to go near a turntable, coaling, watering, and fire-cleaning are all a "straight through" business.

While today it may be thought out-dated, Gateshead shed was far in advance of its time when I ran into it for the first time some twenty-five years ago. I saw here for the first time a series of round sheds, each one with its electric turntable, while the provision for maintenance even today is in the top class.

I liked the N.E. fitters and the way they could tackle a difficult job, and I liked the canteen where you could get anything from a "cuppa" to a full blown dinner, at a time when there wasn't a solitary canteen in any locomotive shed in the whole North British system. Our N.B. officials always seemed to act on the principle that there was something grand about austerity, and treated it almost like a gospel, the theme being the more an engineman lacked in the way of amenities the better he could devote his mind to the job he was paid for. So they did not pander to the desires of the stomach, in any way whatever.

At Gateshead, too, I saw for the first time a "railway institute." It is a massive affair (as is the one at York) and I could hardly believe that this huge building had been erected for the benefit of the staff. Remember at this time Haymarket M.I.C. were still meeting in an old carriage for which we had paid out of our own pocket.

I began to realise the narrow confines to which I had been limited, and talks with my North Eastern pals confirmed this. I spoke to drivers who knew the road between Edinburgh and London, and whose horizon was "big, wide and handsome"—and I began to have ideas. There was no N.B., N.E., or G.N.R now. Maybe some day I'd be penetrating beyond that invisible barrier which stopped my progress at Newcastle.

Maybe it's true that if you wish for a thing hard enough you get it. Nothing will convince me that this isn't true, for it came to pass that the day arrived when I was invited into the "gaffer's" office at Haymarket and John Hutchison, the shed foreman, said.

"Do you know where you're going on Monday, Norman?"

"No."

"You are going to Doncaster to bring back the *Cock a' The North.*" John was all grins.

"Tell me more" I said, mystified, for up to that moment the only *Cock o' The North* I knew as a locomotive was the North British Atlantic of that name. Then John went into details of this new Gresley "P2." It was all a bit "hush-hush" and I was to say nothing to anyone before bringing the engine to Scotland.

Sitting there in an office in Edinburgh I learned for the first time of the "Mikado", the engine which was to revolutionise the train working on the more than severe gradients between Edinburgh and Aberdeen. I was told that it was the biggest express engine of its time, that its valve gear and poppet type valves were something which it was hoped would make all other gears and valves look plain out-of-date. And I was going to Doncaster to bring this engine to beat all engines to Scotland. I managed to get out of that office without actually kissing John Hutchison, but he didn't know how near he was to that fatuous indignity.

This was it! This was to be Gresley's crowning triumph. I can't remember walking home that day, but what did it matter? Since the Gresley Pacifics had come across the Border I had been daft about them. Now and again I'd handled them when the regular driver wasn't available. I knew what they could do. This "Mikado" would be so unique that it would attain standards never before achieved. So I thought.

But as everyone knows, these hopes were never fulfilled, and I took a hand in condemning this engine, for I not only brought her to Scotland, but tested her out in the initial stages on the first stretch of the Edinburgh-Aberdeen run. The "Mikados" were one of Gresley's "near misses" and I suppose there was no more disappointed engineman in Britain than myself that this was so.

I spent two summers bringing Gresley Pacifics and all of the Mikados to Scotland, and think I can lay claim to being the first Haymarket driver to know the road from Edinburgh to Doncaster. Elsewhere I have written about these days when I brought the *Cock o' The North* across the Border, but what I've never told before is how this engine and its type, were the direct means of giving the top link drivers at Haymarket regular engines on the London express trains. If for nothing else than that it brought my Gresley "A3" *Spearmint* and myself into close camaraderie I'm prepared to give a kindly thought to the "Cock," although I learned to dislike the breed through much experience of them.

XIV

"Spearmint" and I

The most glittering period in modern railway history, 1937-1939, had come and gone—the "Coronation"; Gresley's streamliners, a steam locomotive poem in high-speed achievement unsurpassed anywhere else in the world; *Mallard's* 126mph world record; the non-stop "Flying Scotsman," the "Silver Jubilee"—all of them real and satisfying to an engine-man who for years had dreamed of a railway high-speed era. Then another madman ran amok in Germany, and we took the glitter out of the railway scene and assumed the heartbreaking role of the "lines behind the lines."

Plenty has been written about the broad picture of the high-speed era, and the drab years of the war. I do not propose to add to what more qualified people than myself have said. I would, however, like to say something later on a personal note, so let's skip those years meantime and talk of the days which followed.

By the end of the war I was a regular driver in No. 2 link at Haymarket, that is, I was working the Edinburgh-London, Carlisle, Glasgow, Perth, and Aberdeen expresses in rostered rotation. I was also secretary of the staff side of the Local Departmental Committee at Haymarket. The "L.D.C." is the centralised channel of contact between the management and the staff and at this period relations at Haymarket between both couldn't have been better.

For the first time in my career I was working with a shed master who was not only efficient himself, but was prepared to "go to town" in using to the limits the practical efficiency of those who worked with him, and it was this latter urge which made him so different to his predecessors. My previous "gaffers" were efficient enough, but none of them had that intense urge which made them eat, drink, sleep, and think "engine" like the shed master I was now in contact with. He told me when he took over, that he had wanted to come to Haymarket for years, for here he saw a potential for real efficiency which could be practically expressed. He spoke my language, did that lad, and from the word "go" we teamed up.

One day he said: "I've listened to you, and I've read most of what you've written on how officials should act to obtain higher efficiency in locomotive operation. Anybody can talk, and I'm not in agreement with you on many points, in fact I've a good mind, here and now, to call your bluff." That is a good example of how we used to talk to each other, but this time I sensed something more than academical interest in discussing efficiency. I also sensed the reply I was expected to make.

"O.K." I said, "call away, and tell me some more."

"Take our East Coast engines now: how would you produce better punctuality in running, more mileage between shop overhauls, less maintenance costs, and fewer failures?"

He *knew* just the answer I would give to that, so I did not disappoint him. I answered as he expected me to; in fact I answered as I always did when this type of discussion took place.

"Give the top link drivers regular engines, and watch what happens."

As soon as I'd said it I was certain that at last some practical experiment was going to be attempted. This was no mere discussion, it was the first approach I had experienced where a real big honest-to-goodness teaming up could take place with both enginemen and management going all out to disprove a theory which I'd long held to be utterly wrong; namely that the common user engine policy was either efficient or economical where steam locomotives were concerned.

"Let's have the L.D.C. in for a crack on the subject. But I'm warning you it's not as easy as you seem to think," said my "gaffer," so casually that he overdid it.

For that reason the Haymarket L.D.C. spent a good two hours seriously considering every aspect of how top link engines could be rostered, so that their working could be practically performed during the twenty-four hours with two regular drivers to each engine. Next day we had a meeting with the Haymarket shed master.

He outlined the difficulties. Many were routine problems that could be solved locally, but the diagrammed engine working which every shed master receives was not a local business; the diagrams were prepared at York at that time, and were treated like the laws of the Medes and Persians. But they weren't nearly as good as these laws, in fact they were a continual source of irritation to the man who tried to carry out the working. These diagrams were supposed to ensure that each engine was fully utilised for the twenty-four hours, and on paper it looked all right; but no "office wallah" on earth could cater for all the little snags that arose to upset the engine working, and of course, the common user practice fitted in nicely with this sort of thing.

It often happened that two engines instead of one were required to run the early and late turns on the one diagram, because of delays preventing an engine getting to the shed in time to take up its working. All of us at this L.D.C. meeting knew this and all of us knew that to alter the working was a matter for serious consideration, as it meant altering the trains which each link of men were entitled to work according to their seniority, and there was an L.D.C. agreement to this effect. No alteration could be made without consulting the enginemen themselves.

Well, we were out to prove something big, and that two hours discussion hadn't been wasted.

"If you are serious regarding this," we told the "gaffer," "put down your proposals in writing. We will call an open meeting, and back those proposals for all we're worth, providing you too will play. By this we mean that if regular engines are allocated to the top link, you will ensure that, 'come hell or high water,' the drivers will get these engines as their own; that as far as possible the repairs they book will be done; and if at the end of six months this experiment proves a success, then you will endeavour to give the men in as many of the main line links as possible engines of their own, with the engine as well as the man rostered on the duty sheet."

And so it was agreed.

At the open meeting every driver and fireman off duty turned up. It was unique, the most heart-warming experience I've encountered at Haymarket. We said in effect "to hell with those diagrams," and worked out for ourselves train working which would produce top results, not on paper, but in actuality.

The result when put into operation was fantastic. The top link engines started to knock behind them as many as 500 miles a day—each day of the week. The punctuality and time regained north of Newcastle was unbelievable. Everybody in Haymarket from the youngest cleaner to the "gaffer" claimed a share in keeping up the standard, but some of the details can wait. At the end of the six months there was no doubt of the success of the experiment.

One day the shed master invited me into his office. "Well you're going to get your wish," he said. "Number two link are going to get their own Gresleys. There's the list of Haymarket engines, pick your horse."

I didn't hesitate one second. "That's her" I said, "Number 100. I know she's not one hundred per cent. fit at the moment, but let us get together and we'll do our best to achieve that as near as possible."

And so *Spearmint* and I began our partnership.

I said at the conclusion of the last chapter that the *Cock o' the North* and the other "P2s" had a direct bearing on this, and so they had.

I have given the story of how the regular engines came into being at Haymarket. That story is told from *my* angle, but I knew that only one person could make anything like this a practical proposition. That was the Locomotive Running Superintendent. I knew that the decision to allocate regular engines had been made before the shed master could take the action he did, but what I did not know at the time was why it was considered necessary.

I only learned that recently when I decided to write this book.

The fact was that the "P2s," while not popular with enginemen for various reasons, were capable of hauling enormous trains between Aberdeen and Edinburgh, trains like the "Aberdonian" which went on to London. It was necessary that the Gresley Pacifics taking the trains to Newcastle should be in the best of condition. The Locomotive Running Superintendent for the Scottish Area of the L.N.E.R. considered that the best way to achieve this was to give the enginemen regular engines, and one of these engines was *Spearmint.*

I know that it was customary to place high value on a commendation from the Superintendent to the driver. Possibly it could be considered sheer impertinence for the process to come in reverse, but for what it's worth I would like to place on record at least one driver's profound thanks and admiration for a chief and his shed master who thought it worthwhile to allow an engine-man to play some little part in an event which was the means of earning for the top link men at Haymarket the title of "The Elite."

The day after I was told that *Spearmint* and I were to join up, I paid her a visit. She was having a boiler wash-out, and this suited me fine. There was no hurry. So I spent two hours in "looking her over" before going home. She showed all, and more than all the well-known marks of an engine which has fallen a victim to the cult of the common user.

Neglect was shrieking from every pore of her. She was filthily dirty from stem to stern and even to touch the handrails on my climb to the cab was distasteful. To get into the cab at all I had to *kick* the cab doors open, for they were jammed in distorted misalignment. I cleared a place for my feet to stand amongst the litter of coal and muck which covered the floor.

I wiped the driving seat clean of ash dust—at least, I wiped the shreds of leather and protruding horsehair which was supposed to be a padded seat. I sat down and looked around. Mentally I cursed the people who tried to tell me from their office hide-outs that this sort of thing could ever produce efficiency or economy.

I went through my drill of "finding out" and I went about it leisurely. This was my engine now and I wanted to know her. So I lit my pipe and settled down, with not a soul to interrupt. I had driven *Spearmint* on the East Coast expresses as I had driven many other Gresleys—I had sometimes a round half-dozen of them in a week's working on the regular trains—and I knew that below all the signs of neglect there was an honest engine, struggling against odds, and quite surprisingly rising against these odds time and again to do her uncomplaining best. Those odds were going to be shortened in her favour from now on, and I was going to see to it that they were. So I worked my way across the controls and fittings, and there was nothing amiss which did not go down in black and white in the little book I had for this purpose.

I tried the vacuum brake application handle and a touch of my finger sent it into "full on." That meant that the bit of string hanging from the governor casing was needed to tie the handle up and prevent it from shaking "on" whenever the engine started to run. I cut the string off and threw it away. I could sort this out myself.

I operated the gauge column cocks and it needed all the strength I possessed to move them. I took a note of this, and the fact that the gauge glasses were showing a half-inch mourning ring at the bottom. An ooze of yellow-brown lime sediment told me as plain as the writing I'm now doing that the valves inside the gauge columns needed cleaning if they were going to function decently, to say nothing of safely.

The throttle handle was wide open (this to allow air to escape when the boiler was refilled after washing-out). I shut and opened it several times. I positioned it at various openings and touched the handle lightly, but like the brake handle it moved too easily shut. Another "slaister" of lime ooze at the throttle gland pointed to the cure for this and again the little book came into use.

I reached up and cut off the string which was acting as a whistle pull. That also went into the book with a note about the filthy pressure gauge and the vacuum brake and steam heater gauges, along with the missing screws which should have been holding them tight to the stormboard. I did not need to try the injector steam keys. All the signs told me that as soon as the boiler started to generate steam both steam keys would start to drip water—the marks were there plain to see—and this was also evident on the blower and vacuum steam keys.

From where I sat writing it all down I stretched out a hand, and pulled the gravity sand lever. It only moved half its travel, so evidently a stone was jamming one of the valves; I'd have to test this out by disconnection until I found which one was sticking. I'd need assistance to do this, as well as a few other things that needed attention, and that assistance was grinning up at me when I looked over the side.

It was one of my boys, a young fireman whom I'd licked into shape when he joined as a cleaner.

"Just come up, Ginger, I can use you," I said, and Ginger, ever willing, came swarming up the cab steps.

"Sit there and do what I tell you when I holler," I said. I got down on the ground, slipped underneath *Spearmint* to make sure there was no one working on her or that any of the bits were dismantled, and once this was verified, started to "holler" to Ginger. With the patience of the young who tolerate without understanding the queernesses of the older generation Ginger acted as my slave until I was satisfied.

I satisfied myself about a lot of things with Ginger's help. From the water-scoop under the tender to the relief cocks at the cylinder ends I learned all I wanted to know, including the bits that needed oil to make the reverser work without my rupturing myself trying to get it back into gear.

At last I released the willing red-headed one and told him as a reward: "Some day if you are good, and on the spare, and can shovel coals to get the fire the same colour as your hair, I'll let you come with me as a fireman on the finest engine in Britain."

"What engine is that?"

"Her number's 100, her name's *Spearmint,* and you're standing looking at her."

Ginger gave one look at the engine, and his reply was laconic. "I'll believe it when I come firing to you", he grinned.

I may say that he did make that trip with me a year later, and I asked the "gaffer" specially to put him on the job when my regular mate was required for a driving spell one day.

So I spent my first two hours with *Spearmint,* for which incidentally I was receiving no pay, but it was rewarding nonetheless, even if it did cost the railway a completely new set of corks and oil trimmings which I took out and pitched into the fire-box. The corks were useless, the trimmings were mere pretences and were just as useful in the firebox as they were *in situ*—functionless.

As I went round my engine from tender to engine buffers I ruthlessly and relentlessly put down every mortal thing I could find which called for attention by the fitters, blacksmith, joiner, boilersmith, and brake blocker. When I finished I stood over on the other road where I could take in *Spearmint* from one end to the other. She was standing dejected-looking, with a dirty and bedraggled look on her like a lady run to seed.

But I didn't see the dirt. Somewhere below that glutinous mess was green paint and smooth buffed steel. I'd seen it when she came new to Haymarket. I'd see it again—and I'd see that so long as we ran together she would never again look dejected. Then I sauntered off to spend another thirty minutes filling three pages of a foolscap size repair book.

After that, I thought, I had better see Jock Gray, for he would faint if I didn't warn him about that little lot of "repairs." But Jock grinned like the devil when he saw me at the door of his office.

"You've been having quite a time, haven't you? I saw you, and you needn't say it," he greeted me. "You've put enough in the book to keep us busy for a week, I expect, but it's only three days before you get her on the Perth, and that's all I can afford. I knew you would be after me, so it's all arranged; she's 'shopped' till Monday. Come and see how we're getting on tomorrow."

That was Mechanical Foreman Jock Gray all over. With a shed full of common user high capacity engines, all needing attention all the time, Jock could and did find time to have the jobs done when a driver took the trouble to book them properly. I had worked in close contact with him all the war years, and never once found him unwilling to back up a driver by practical assistance if the driver on his side was prepared to talk sense.

I'm hoping to show how as this yarn proceeds.

Actually the three pages of "repairs" I had booked for *Spearmint* weren't so deadly, and Jock was exaggerating when he estimated a week to do them. What I had booked were (more or less) the "scratches" which, while evidence of neglect, did not stop the engine from running. *Spearmint* was due for a "periodical examination" and while this was going on most of the entries I made in the repair book were "chalked off."

So when I turned out on Monday to work the 7.40am Edinburgh to Perth, *Spearmint's* pistons and valve rings had been renewed, the exhaust ports cleaned, and the throttle valve and other steam jobs given attention. Somehow the harassed foreman cleaner had managed to clean a little of the grime from the obvious parts.

I was early, but in spite of that it took me almost all the time I had to get the engine ready. The kit or rather lack of it had to be gathered together as a preliminary to anything being done at all. This meant trying keys on nuts to see they really fitted the parts for which they were intended, exchanging or discarding the useless, obtaining a new footplate brush, coal hammer, and pail, seeing that the lamps, oil cans, and "pouries" were really in good condition, to say nothing of the fire irons, shovels, and so on. My mate and I spent quite a while before we were satisfied, and nearly drove the store-keeper "round the bend" before we finished.

Before we left Haymarket, *Spearmint* was equipped with more new kit than I had seen for a long time on any one engine. But we left most of it stowed in the pail. The tool box was swimming half an inch deep in water with an oily scum floating on top like all the colours of the rainbow. So we went to Perth. There is nothing remarkable in a Gresley Pacific's performance on this train. At that time the load on starting from Edinburgh was only half that which *Spearmint* was capable of handling, and was further reduced on the way to Perth. It is a short run, and a Gresley (even in bad condition) could do it on its head.

The value of this job to the driver with his own engine was the reasonable time between his arrival and return working, and (so far as I was concerned) the fact that you could park your engine at the end of a loop and work away uninterruptedly. Right now I would like a word with the economists who see a chance to exercise their talent when they spot a spare hour where an engine is shown on the diagrammed working as doing nothing for an hour or so between trains. It is during those supposed-to-be idle hours, that a real engine-man gives attention to his engine, and possibly saves a good deal more real cash than the "paper economy" shown by the hour taken from his daily diagram, and marked by the economist— "unproductive" time.

Unproductive time! Ye gods! if they had seen what happened in the time we had at our disposal that week at Perth. While my mate was swabbing out the tool box and making it fit to house tools and oil cans (which did not leak), while he was doing this and knocking some of the filth off the cab, I was on the ground with the cab doors and a hammer straightening them to the shape they were supposed to be; and you've no idea what can be done in this respect using a rail as an anvil. These were first essentials.

Once we got some semblance of sense into head lamps and gauge lamps, cleaned the gauge glass protectors so that the water looked like water and not a misty, ghostly movement "seen through a glass darkly," it was time for me to give attention to things not normally looked at on the common user engines.

Again I'd like to say a word to the people who think that the common user principle is an economy on railway steam engines. I could almost guarantee to find on any common user engine which has been running for a few months a dozen oiling points at the very least which have never received a drop of lubrication.

This was the case with *Spearmint*. I made a long pricker out of a 12 gauge steel wire pin, and bit by bit cleared the holes on the brake hanger and laminated spring pins. The oil holes on all of them were solid with dirt, and as a result the pins were being worn a good deal faster than they should have been with proper attention, and that is the sort of thing the common user principle breeds.

But there's more to it than that. As I say I cleared all the oil holes which were never used as such, and this included tender as well as engine, and a lot more than merely spring and brake hanger pins. And as I slowly worked my way round my engine I was noting things—noting, for instance, how the driving box wedges needed adjusting.

Again, the common user advocate should know that I blamed this lack of proper adjustment for the broken exhaust injector pipe which was discovered when I opened the cock at the smokebox. That "palaver" meant that *Spearmint* was burning a good deal more coal than she needed to, if the exhaust injector had been working.

But why go on? A month after I got her, *Spearmint* was holding up her head, shining from stem to stern, every mortal thing functioning to perfection. And she wasn't the only one. Nor was it outward show. Thanks to Jock Gray she had as near a perfect steam action as any Gresley I've heard exhausting. Let me give you just one example of what took place.

I wasn't entirely satisfied with the steam action the first few weeks, and it took me a while to spot where it could be cured. I thought it was the centre engine, and discussed it with Jock. It was little enough that was wrong, but I wasn't prepared to have even a little thing wrong if by any means it could be cured.

It was near Jock's lunch time, and he needn't have bothered until a more opportune moment, but that wasn't his way. *Spearmint* was due out on her train within an hour, and that hour was devoted by Jock (aided and abetted by myself) to trial and error testing, and the fitting of various thicknesses of the little metal distance pieces behind the left valve rod, until one no thicker than the paper on which this book is printed brought about the desired result. Jock was an hour late home for his lunch, and possibly Mrs. "Jock" would have something to say about spoiled food, but he left me grinning like a Cheshire cat.

That is the sort of thing which the regular engine in the hands of regular drivers bred.

The common user principle as applied to railway locomotives has never really produced efficiency or economy in spite of the specious arguments in its favour and possibly this can be more readily understood by a statement of an actual fact which was clearly demonstrated at Haymarket.

According to the "book" the mileage expected from a Gresley in the days of which I write was 80-82,000 miles between workshop overhauls. (This was under the L.N.E.R. system, and should not be confused with the L.M.S.R. system, which produced apparently impressive figures until you analysed just how they were compiled). It was the exception rather than the rule that the common user engine ever put in the mileage laid down; from my own experience I felt that by the time they had reached the 60,000 mark they had reached a stage where they badly needed a works overhaul.

In the hands of regular men the Gresley Pacifics seldom required a works overhaul before they had run 90-100,000 miles, while some of them were running anything up to 140,000 miles from the time they left Doncaster works until they returned—not only working a train, but in such conditions that the works people actually questioned the mileage figures given. As my chief said to me when discussing the effect of the regular engine policy, "It proved what I have always asserted, 'wear and tear' should never be an accepted slogan." I'm willing to admit "wear," but with locomotives properly maintained and looked after "tear" should not be evident.

The condition of the Haymarket Gresleys bore this out after many years, not only mechanically, but in boiler "wear" as well.

XV

Performance Plus

There was a distinct difference between my attitude to *Spearmint* and that of the drivers to whom I occasionally fired. All of the main line drivers at Haymarket (or for that matter any depot on the North British) had their regular engines. Those men usually threw a cloak of mystery around their steeds. This indicated that no one knew how to drive their particular engines except themselves.

If by any chance another engineman *did* get their engine for a day he would be sure to heat it, or break something, or do any of a dozen different things which the regular driver knew how to avoid. It was all a matter of profound secrecy, and I've seen two drivers coming to fisticuffs after the one accused the other of mishandling an engine.

To me, even as a youngster, this was pure nonsense. If an engine was so delicate that special care and attention was required to keep it running and only the regular driver had the "know-how" on this, then it was logical to assume that this was a reflection on him—a reflection on him for not curing the disease properly, rather than have a semi-invalid running the road, which the first breath of cold wind would send into "hospital," possibly creating a lot of trouble for shed staff and the bloke who took the "rap" for "mismanagement of the engine."

So my crack to any engineman who drove *Spearmint* during my absence from duty was: "Drive her how you like, she can take it." I'm pleased to record that *Spearmint* whole-heartedly agreed with me. I was only too pleased to see my engine being used to the limit; that was the main object for which we had obtained regular engines. And *Spearmint* was not only fit to "take it," but revelled in doing so.

During the years I drove her, and after a few of the delicate bits were made sound, I never once had to answer for any delay to the trains I regularly worked, "due to locomotive causes." Rather was it the reverse. She pulled back hours and hours of lost time on the Anglo-Scottish expresses, and on many occasions got tough treatment.

There was, for instance, that night in 1947.

The snow had been falling for days. All over Britain trains were being held up for hours and sometimes days. I was on one of the

London night trains from Edinburgh, the "Night Scotsman" if I remember rightly. We had some 500 tons on.

No one could give me much "gen" on what to expect on the road, for the snow was falling so quickly that in minutes it could convert a comparatively clear stretch of line into a series of impedimenta to free running, but I wasn't worrying much. It would be easy compared to the run to Perth I had just three days previously, when we were snowed up for a solid twelve hours at Kelty. There would be nothing like this on the East Coast to Newcastle.

"What's the betting that we reach Newcastle on time?" I said to Jimmy Stewart, my mate. What prompted me to say that I don't know, unless it was the ever-present urge to "make every difficulty an opportunity," or maybe just vanity about *Spearmint* which made for "brag"; or again just because I knew Jimmy.

If you don't know Jimmy, just think of a bulldog with the pleasantest grin imaginable, a ginger head, and the build of a pocket Hercules. His main off-duty relaxation was to go the rounds of the boxing booths at any of the fairs which came within his orbit, knocking out unwary "pro's," and collecting an honest pound or two with a calm insouciance that never even disturbed his remarkable cheerfulness.

A battle of any kind was meat and drink to him, and I used to tell him (much to his puzzlement) that his proper environment was with the Three Musketeers, swashbuckling through a previous century.

"There's nothing to hinder us running time. Don't let a wee drop snow beat you," was how he treated a near blizzard. While I mentally agreed with him, I refused to prophesy.

We struck the open country soon enough, and then the battle commenced. Normally *Spearmint* would run this section with no more than 15 per cent. cut-off and less than half the throttle open. That night I shoved the throttle wide open, and to keep up the speed wound her out to 30 per cent. Just, *but only just,* we ran to the timetable on that particular section. I knew from this first try-out (and so did Jimmy) that if it needed all that on this stretch, it would need a darned sight more on the road which lay ahead.

"Are we still going to run to time, Jim?" I sang out.

That 30 per cent. hadn't been easy on him, and I knew how gruelling any more could be on a fireman if it was kept up for long periods at a time. I also knew that within a few minutes I would be flogging *Spearmint* along at 40, 45, and whatever more was anybody's guess. And so did Jimmy.

His reply to my shout was to take off his dungaree jacket and pitch it into the coatbox. He gave a jerk of his head. "Come on," he grinned, "there's nothing to it."

Two minutes later I wound her out to 40, then the pointer went to 45, and on the last three miles to Grantshouse it was at full forward. *Spearmint* was nearly blowing the rocks asunder with the explosions from her exhaust, and lifting chunks out of the fire and hurling them sky-high.

"They'll be coming down when we return," said Jimmy, looking at the pyrotechnics coming chimney-thick. The little devil was actually enjoying himself.

There was no use thinking of an "easy" on the five miles of downhill if we were going to maintain time. Down we went with the throttle still wide open, but I managed to pull her back to 30 per cent. cut-off. That was the last time the reverser pointer saw 30 on that run. I never got it to less than 35 per cent. the whole way to Newcastle. Most of the way it was at 40/45 per cent. and quite a few times in full fore gear.

One of these latter times was a few miles north of Chevington, where the layer of snow was thicker and was acting like a "sand-drag" in its effort to slow *Spearmint* down. I would have liked a moving picture of our progress through that stretch. We were running fast, and two huge gushes of snow were spurting from either side of *Spearmint,* almost smokebox high, with a cataract caught in the gale we were creating and smacking up against the cab front like a gun barrage. But *Spearmint* just tore through these miles regardless.

We did *not* arrive at Newcastle on time, but there was no disgrace in losing the handful of minutes we were behind our schedule. In point of fact, it wasn't all the fault of the snow that we didn't make time. Our tender was all but stripped of coal, our tank was as low as safety allowed, and our effort was really governed by this, although it's questionable whether I'd have had the heart to flog *Spearmint* any more than I had done, even given unlimited coal and water. It was brutal treatment to give any willing engine. It was ruthlessly merciless on Jimmy as well, but neither of them showed that they thought so.

When we stopped at Newcastle, I stepped off to have a look at *Spearmint.* There was hardly a bit of her visible for snow; even the spokes of her driving wheels were forming "reinforcing" to the snow, which in spite of their pounding progress had managed to cling and make of the wheels solid white discs.

But—and this is the main reason for telling about the remorseless hammering I gave *Spearmint* that night—there was no sign of this on one part of the engine. The big ends were as cold as the snow which clung to the static bits around them. There wasn't even a "running heat" on the boxes. After standing that run, I think I was justified in telling any driver who worked her in my absence, "drive her how you like, she can take it."

As for Jimmy Stewart, when he got back into the cab after cleaning the banked-up snow between the tender and carriage to allow him to uncouple, he merely remarked between swigs of hot tea: "Well, I've called you many things in my time, but after this, you're name's 'Basher McKillop'."

Although I earned the name of "Basher" on that run with Jimmy Stewart, I think I can say with truth that never once have I asked an engine *(any* engine I have ever driven, never mind *Spearmint)* to exert herself needlessly, and after the hectic run I've just described I feel that it's fair enough to give a few details of the treatment *Spearmint* got under normal circumstances, when the sun or the moon were shining in benevolence on our progress.

In every way I could think up I lightened her work, and this meant more than the usual routine. For instance, I seldom left Edinburgh on the head of an express train without satisfying myself that the brakes on that train were *fully* released. I knew that to depend entirely on what the vacuum brake gauge told me in the cab could quite easily be deceiving, so when we "tied on" and everything was in order, I seldom missed walking the *whole* length of the train having a look at the brake blocks.

Dozens of times I've found one or two of them not fully released, and pulled the release chain which did the trick. Sometimes it was little enough friction this would have caused, a little more than the weight of the block on the wheel, but even curing that was worth the half-mile stroll which is about the total distance you walk to examine a fifteen-coach train, and return to the engine.

About lubrication I was as bad as the lad who oiled the strap holes of his cycle tool bag. I saw to it that every bit which moved, or rubbed against another bit, did so with a film of oil to keep them apart.

Remember what I said about Perth? Well one of the most noticeable differences between that outward run and the return trip was the smoothness we achieved going back after I'd given a "lick of oil" to the "rubbing blocks" between engine and tender. My mate was amazed at the difference it made. Instead of a harsh, almost "lifting" action as we ran over the rail joints, there was a smooth almost imperceptible motion to the cab floor.

I was not supposed to touch the mechanical lubricator (officially, that is) but I couldn't see any fitter knowing what *Spearmint* needed as well as I did, and the lubricator pumps were adjusted to her liking, not to a formula which had been worked out on paper. Any thinking engineman knows that it's just as realistic to tell a human being what to eat and drink to retain health, as it is to say the same to an engine, without knowing something about their individual characteristics.

It was the same on the road. My favourite train was the 10am Edinburgh to London, the "Flying Scotsman." I have a water-colour painting by my good friend Mr. O. S. Nock showing *Spearmint* on the head of this train, and every time I look at that scene with a sparkling sea, green grass and brown cliffs, with the train and engine adding the finishing touch in shining harmony, I'm reminded of the hundreds of times I've experienced the reality, and know that despite its completeness, there is one thing that picture just cannot tell. That is the utter satisfaction it gives a driver to have all this, and a well-cared for and contented engine as company in his enjoyment.

The spot where that painting shows *Spearmint* and the "Scottie" in full flight is nearly sixty miles from her starting point, and when we were together she did that in sixty minutes. She is shown with a long white plume of steam barely higher than the roofs of the carriages, and that's how it should be, because the throttle is nearly closed, and has been that way for a good few miles. The reversing lever pointer is in 15 per cent., there's hardly more than a few inches of fire covering the fire-bars, and she, my mate, and myself are comfortably enjoying the moment.

Right from the start at Edinburgh there's been an almost prim regard in precise attention to detail operation. The cab is like a new pin, and my mate has given the slightest of moves to an injector steam key packing nut, because the faintest sign of moisture appears to mar its polished surface. Although there's little fire in the "box," he's in no hurry to lift the shovel. He knows that for at least five minutes there will be hardly enough blast on the fire to be felt, never mind burn the coal.

Not until I open the throttle ever so little does he throw in the minimum number of shovel-fulls to set the flames, white hot, licking at the brick arch. The injector hadn't put a drop of water into the boiler during that five minutes and the first *easy* three and a half miles, and our train weighs 450 tons.

Even when the throttle is pulled wide-open there's no hurry to pile in coal, for that "wide-open" doesn't mean a great deal in blast when the port opening is so small that the steam is cut off when the piston has travelled only a fraction of its full stroke. But it is hot steam, and a little goes a long way; moreover it's hot steam, mainly because I see to it that every boiler tube is meticulously clean. Like the advertisement, both *Spearmint* and I are great believers in "inner cleanliness" to give that fresh feeling.

And *Spearmint is* as fresh as a daisy. Even the fairly formidable climbs are made in the fluent free loping fashion that characterised her namesake, a famous racehorse, and there's little or no sign of effort as she breasts the slopes with never more on one of them than 20 per cent. and on all the others a mere 15 per cent, cut-off.

Long before coming to the point shown in Mr. Nock's picture I had tapped the throttle shut until the steam chest pressure gauge registered just under 90, not because *Spearmint* needed as much as that, but to keep the exhaust injector working (it works on live steam after the exhaust steam drops below 90 lbs. pressure). The moment the injector is shut off prior to the point shown in the picture, the throttle is nearly shut, with no more than 30 lbs. of pressure doing the job.

Remember what I said about that throttle handle? It didn't shake shut now when we were running. The throttle gland was so adjusted that I could set the handle and maintain any pressure I liked to within one pound registered on the steam chest pressure gauge. This stood for the brake application handle as well, which I'm now reaching for as we approach Berwick and I brake for the 30mph curve. No bits of string holding this now. It was just a simple matter of packing and adjusting the spindle gland and nuts, and the "weight" of the handle was suited to my natural requirements.

It is a fact which I've long known, that like a cricket bat, a tennis racquet, a golf club, or a fencing foil, the "weight," the balance, and the "feel" of an engine's controls are as important to efficient operation as are these implements of sport to their top class wielders.

As with the controls, I'd made it my business to see that *Spearmint* wasn't running with anything to cramp her free action, and as shortly she "tip-toedthrough-the-tulips" down into Goswick, and round the bend to touch a flashing 80 on the straight before Beal, it was all being done with the minimum of effort, no sideways roll, or for that matter any motion except straight forward. It was just a matter of proper weight on the springs, and judicious adjustment of the driving box wedges, with all of Jock Gray's knowledge and experience of what was just right for a Gresley Pacific to be happy at her work.

That was *Spearmint's* normal life when she and I were together. On occasion I asked much from her, and never once did she fail to respond. In return I tried not to let her down, and am sure I succeeded, for she told me so in unmistakable fashion. In case you don't believe me, I'd like to give an actual case to prove that not only *Spearmint* could "talk" to her driver, but that in point of fact it's a habit which all the Gresley Pacifics share.

I would like to quote an actual instance of this, of which I've written before, and which another writer thought worthy of inclusion in his book. What hasn't been written before, however, is one of the performances which this same engine put up when a skilled observer was on the footplate to log the run. I feel that both the run and the log are well worth including in this chapter, as proof that what was done with *Spearmint* could be done, and was in fact done, with any Gresley Pacific which teamed up with a regular crew.

I have repeatedly asserted that there is no such thing as a bad Gresley Pacific engine and by that I mean the locomotives built by Gresley as Pacific types, not some conversion, such as the "P2s" became. Now and again to refute this rather sweeping statement, my colleagues produce chapter and verse of poor performance by a Pacific and say, in effect: "What about your Gresley now? This one's a dud." My retort to that is; "Give her to me as a regular engine, let me hear what *she's* got to say about it, and not till then will I really believe what you say to her discredit."

On one occasion I got the opportunity of having this experience. I rather think the occasion was rigged by the Shedmaster at Haymarket who, as I've mentioned in the previous chapter, liked to "call my bluff," as he put it. In any case it gave me the chance to give *Hyperion* a new reputation, and her reputation was really bad when I took her over for a month or two when *Spearmint* was at

Doncaster for her works overhaul. Before I took over No. 60037 *Hyperion* I had heard all about her. She wouldn't run, she wouldn't steam freely, in fact there was hardly an item in the calendar of bad performance which had not been levelled against her.

This was borne out in the first miserable week we spent together, when I had to leather her unmercifully to run a night East Coast express to time. There was little or no opportunity of doing anything to the engine on this turn, and I had to possess my soul in patience until the following week, when on the daylight run to Perth and back, I could *see* as well as *hear* and try to understand what was ailing this "A3."

How she was cured has as I have already said, been told in that other book, and I don't need to repeat the details here. Briefly it can be stated, however, that inside a short period *Hyperion* was like a different engine. She ran like a bird, steamed to perfection, and I had the satisfaction of graciously consenting to relinquish her for a day (or rather a night) so that she could run the Royal Train.

That story has, as I have said, been told in detail before, and a log of a run by *Hyperion* on the up afternoon "Scotsman" given to point the moral. That log was good, but the return one was better in my opinion, and as neither the story of the down run nor the log of it has been published before, I would like to give my version of it here.

As can be seen from the log which Ronald I. Nelson compiled sitting on 60037, our start out of Newcastle was sticky. Signals were cramping our style, and it was a good two and a half miles from Newcastle before I could really let him see what this supposed "dud" engine was capable of doing. By following the log you also will be able to appreciate it.

All the way to Forest Hall is uphill and *Hyperion* wasn't harassed. I knew the sticky start had cost us a few minutes, and I knew also where I was going to get them back, so we took it easy (notice that 12 per cent. cut-off at Cramlington) to slide through Morpeth a good 10mph slower than required without touching the brake. That was after a "drift" of three miles and an example of using the road, rather than the brake.

Neither *Hyperion* nor I was in a hurry. There was no use "bashing" on just to get signal checks from the train ahead; those would come soon enough at one of the worst places on the road, and then it would be time to let Mr. Nelson see how time was regained with discretion. If you notice just where we *did* get nearly stopped by signals at Alnmouth, you will also notice that for almost three miles prior to that, *Hyperion's* regulator was almost closed and she was notched up to 12 per cent.

Alnmouth lies in a hollow and ahead are five miles of bank mostly of 1 in 200. We were four minutes down, and should have been a good deal more according to the signal checks we had received, but still we weren't worrying.

Now look at what this engine did on that long bank, and remember that just a few weeks before she was being condemned right and left. Remember also that had we not been checked by signals we would have had a flying start on the bank at 60 instead of 10mph Without check, I reckoned always on allowing 5 to 5½ minutes from Alnmouth to Little Mill. Yet *Hyperion* waltzed up this stretch in a little over 6 minutes, and as you can see was in 25 per cent. cut-off for the last two miles of the climb, very quickly reduced to 15, then 12 per cent. for the fast, tightly scheduled twelve miles to Beal.

That near stop at Alnmouth at the foot of a long bank had cost us little or nothing in the way of lost time. We passed Belford, our next passing point, just under four-and-a-half minutes down, and still we weren't harassing ourselves. Notice the "drift" with the regulator no more than a quarter open for two miles before the water troughs at Lucker: see how the speed has petered out from 78 to 58mph That's what you can do with a *good* engine to lift the water comfortably, quite apart from the 60mph restriction very sensibly imposed when crossing the troughs.

Notice also on the log how that 12 per cent. cut-off persists and see how the recovery time has been utilised to get us back on our schedule long before the Border is crossed, and the demarcation line between the North Eastern Region and the Scottish Region passed at Marshall Meadows. There was a good reason for this—at least, a good personal reason.

We had left Newcastle on time, but had been subjected to signal checks which would have justified *Hyperion* being at least seven minutes to the bad, or, if you take four minutes of recovery time allowed from Belford, she would not have been disgraced in passing over the Border Bridge at least three minutes down. As it was, she passed into the Scottish Region a minute and three quarters ahead of schedule, and everybody was pleased. So there was no writing for signalmen in making out reports as to why the train was delayed, no time wasted by loco. inspectors asking me, questions, and, above all, no time wasted by me giving either verbal or written explanations.

For it is a fact that while the writing "bug" has bitten me for as long as I can remember, I detest useless writing, and would rather run than write reports any day. As I well knew, whenever the nose of my engine passed Marshall Meadows box, my passing time would be flashed to Edinburgh, and quite a few people would want to know all about the lost minutes.

This of course isn't or never has been my sole reason for consistently regaining lost time if I could do so within reason, for I realise there are many arguments for and against it from an engineman's point of view, but the only thing which I bar in pulling back the lost minutes is *(a)* I refuse to exceed any speed restriction, or *(b)* I will *not*, repeat *not*, abuse an engine or "kill" my fireman to regain a minute or two.

This run was no exception to my general rule, and as can be seen from the log *Hyperion* did the trip "on her head." Ronald Nelson, a top expert in logging a run, calculates that the net time taken was 130½ minutes for the 124.4 miles from Newcastle to Edinburgh—and that with a fresh wind blowing, to say nothing of the rain and darkness of a bleak February night.

This log also brings to light one or two things which only the driver can see in his minds' eye. Look at the log again and notice that remark at Widdrington about "slight easing" and the three-quarter opening of the regulator; see how the speed has dropped from 73 to 68mph to Chevington. That slight easing of the speed was a self-imposed speed restriction. It pin-points another angle of locomotive operation which I've always (as an engineman driving high-speed trains) taken into consideration in my timing. There are bits of the track which are perfectly safe to run at the top limit allowed, but are not as comfortable as they might be. On these stretches I make a habit of finding out just what speed could cut out the little roll or oscillation, and that "slight easing" here and there gave the engine, the crew, and the passengers, a better time, by a continued and unbroken rhythm, which, while maybe not apparent to the casual eye, was to me a most important item in running a train.

As can also be seen on this log, *Hyperion* arrived in Edinburgh three minutes ahead of time. In other words she did not require the "recovery time" allowed in the running. This, if anything, proves what can be done with a supposedly "dud" Gresley Pacific, for on that first week we spent together I had to flog the engine to get her in to time, using every minute of the recovery time, and having no excuses in the way of signal checks to salve either her conscience or mine.

Yes! I think I'm safe in saying there are no bad Gresley Pacifics.

7-3pm NEWCASTLE-EDINBURGH

Engine: "A3" class 4-6-2 No. 60037 *Hyperion* | *Load:* 10 cars, 318 tons tare, 335 tons gross | *Driver:* N. McKillop *Fireman:* G. Brown (Haymarket) | Inspector: I. Cunningham (Waverley)

Distance miles		Schedule	Actual min	Actual sec	Speed mph	Boiler pressure lb/sq in	Steam chest pressure lb/sq in	Regulator	Cut-off per ct
0.0	NEWCASTLE	0	0	0	–	205	100	⅜	65
	Sigs.			10		200	105	½	35
0.6	Manors East	–	2	51	–	200	0	Shut	35
	Sigs. check								
2.6	Benton Bank	–	9	53	–	200	185	Full	25
5.0	Forest Hall	–	14	07	37	210	200	Ful	20
5.9	Killingsworth	–	15	21	45½	205	195	Ful	17
7.7	Annitsford	–	17	26	60	205	195	Ful	15
9.9	Cramlington	–	19	47	56½	205	190	Ful	12
11.5	Plessey	–	21	29	62½	200	187	Ful	12
13.9	Stannington	–	23	34	75	200	55	¼	12
16.6	MORPETH	24	27	02	30	200	185	Ful	25
18.5	Pegswood	–	29	41	49½	210	200	Ful	18
20.2	Longhirst	–	31	20	67	215	200	Ful	18
23.2	Widdrington	–	34	04	73	215	200	Ful	15
	(Slight easing-track in bad repair)				200	150	¾		
25.6	Chevington	–	36	09	68	200	185	Ful	12
28.5	Acklington	–	38	46	72½	200	185	Ful	12
31.9	Warkworth	–	41	29	77½ max.	200	30	¼	12
	Sigs.			10	195		180	Ful	35
34.8	ALNMOUTH	42	46	09	27	200	185	Ful	28
37.5	Longhoughton	–	49	54	47½	210	195	Ful	25
39.4	Little Mill	–	52	26	48	205	190	Pal	25
				62½	200		185	Ful	15
41.0	Milepost 41	–	54	13	59	200	185	Ful	12
43.0	Christon Bank	–	55	56	76	205	160	¾	12
46.0	Chathill	–	58	14	81	210	165	¾	12
47.1	Newham	–	59	04	78	205	60	¼	12
49.2	Lucker	–	61	07	58	205	190	Ful	12
51.6	BELFORD	59*	63	29	61½	205	95	Ful	12

Distance miles		Schedule	Actual min	Actual sec	Speed mph	Boiler pressure lb/sq in	Steam chest pressure lb/sq in	Regulator	Cut-off per ct
54.9	Smeafield	–	66	26	74	210	200	Ful	12
58.6	Beal	–	69	21	83½	200	190	Ful	12
60.8	Goswick	–	70	59	82	205	192	Ful	15
63.5	Scremerston	–	73	08	70½	200	187	Ful	15
64.5	Milepost 64½	–	74	00	66	200	55	¼	15
65.7	Tweedmouth	–	75	23	50	200	55	¼	15
66.9	BERWICK	78*	76	52	40	195	185	Full	25
68.0	Marshall Meadows	80	78	15	47½	205	195	Full	25
	(Temporary bridge and land slide slacks)								
78.1	Reston Jc.	98	93	19	–				
83.1	Grantshouse	115	110	11	–				
87.9	Cockburnspath	–	120	39	55	200	80	⅜	12
90.6	Innerwick	–	123	22	68½	190	155	⅝	12
93.1	Oxwellmains	–	125	43	61½	197	50	¼	12
95.2	DUNBAR	130	128	11	54	195	180	Full	15
97.4	Beltonford	–	130	27	60	215	205	Full	15
99.4	Milepost 25	–	132	33	57½	215	205	Full	15
01.0	East Linton	–	134	22	53½	210	175	¾	12
03.6	East Fortune	–	137	07	64½	215	200	Full	12
06.6	Drem Jc.	142	140	03	58	205	195	Full	12
09.6	Aberlady Jc.	–	143	23	53	200	155	⅝	12
11.2	Longniddry Jc.	147*	145	08	61½	195	150	⅝	12
	(Easy running-recovery time allowed)								
18.3	Monktonhall .Jc. p.w.s.								
P		159*	154	39	–				
					20	190	130	½	25
21.4	Portobello	165	161	26	40	177	120	½	15
22.6	Piershill Jc.	–	163	09	41½	200	190	Full	25
23.5	Abbeyhill Jc.	–	165	03	25	190	175	Full	25
24.4	WAVERLEY	171	167	54	–	–	–	–	–

Net time 130½ mins. (Without allowance for easy running after Drem). | Left Newcastle on time, arrived Waverley 3 mins. early.
Moderate south-westerly wind, freshening, and rain after Tweedmouth. | 4 min. recovery time margin on sections marked*.
Equivalent drawbar horsepower at Little Mill 1,412.

XVI
War and all That

The war years brought a veritable hotch-potch of strange engines to Haymarket—American 2-8-0s, G.N. "D1" 4-4-0, and those (to me) strange Great Eastern "B12" 4-6-0s with their water pump on the footplate and part of the apparatus strapped on the top of their boiler. It was inevitable that they should be christened "hikers" straight off.

I brought the first "hiker" to Haymarket and must say that for such old engines they were remarkably in advance of their time. They had back and front air sanders to which the air was admitted according to the position of the reversing gear, i.e., if the gear was in "fore" the front sands operated, if in back gear the rear sands worked. The sandbox lids were fitted with rubber washers, a detail refinement that even today would prove valuable.

The distance from the tender shovel hole to the fire-door was the longest I've seen on any engine. I was told that firing shovels with six-foot shafts should have been standard equipment on them, but we never saw these shovels, and to fire them the fireman had to take quite a promenade.

As for the driver, it was a sheer impossibility for him to brake his train and still look over the side of the cab to see where he was in the black-out. This was important where station platforms were normally on the side away from where the driver was positioned. The "B12s" were "right hand drive" and the distance from the brake application handle and the edge of the cab side window was fifty-one inches. No normal arm could reach that far.

They wouldn't steam between telegraph poles as one driver said in disgust, but they had a peculiar "saver" in the fact that the lower the steam pressure became, the better they seemed able to maintain the vacuum in the train. An idea of their decrepit condition when they came to Haymarket can be gauged from the fact that when I opened the smokebox door of one to see if I could spot the cause for the poor steaming, I found the "petticoat" which extends from the chimney to above the blast-pipe rusted and full of holes.

I tested them out to see if they would do for our Edinburgh-Glasgow expresses, and while I reported that they just could not do the job, I was more than impressed with what they *did* do.

I've already said this forty-seven miles of nearly flat road is difficult to run because there is no "let-up" for an engine which needs an occasional "shutoff" to allow her to get her breath back if she's short of steam. Well, those "B12s", with no more than 100 lb. pressure and sometimes even less than that, kept eleven bogie carriages going with little loss of time on a very tight schedule. They could run like a deer. Later, when it was seen how useless it was trying to get real work out of them, they went north, where I believe the old Great North of Scotland works at Inverurie did a grand job in making them fit to run trains sensibly.

Of the "Yankees" I did not see very much on the class of trains I was working but now and again when schedules went "hay-wire" I ran an occasional ammunition train with them. Those trains were abnormally heavy as a rule, and with a British engine would have required a pilot on some of the banks. Not so with these enormously strong products of Uncle Sam. I believe they could have taken any *two* of our normal trains and never turned a hair. I can't recollect having the throttle any further than a quarter open on the heaviest trains.

They weren't nice engines to ride on above thirty miles an hour. In fact I rather had the "wind-up" when they got into speed, not for the bad riding, but for the way the reversing lever tried its darndest to pull the quadrant and its fittings from the boiler end to which it was fixed. Of all the unsafe things to do in locomotive design this was the most risky which has ever come under my notice. If that fixture had been pulled out (and I heard this actually happened in England) the fellow standing in line with the resulting stream of scalding water would stand a poor chance of surviving. I didn't want to experience this sort of thing, and cannily took avoiding action when on board an "Americano."

After seeing this sort of thing I wasn't much surprised to see a mixture of good and bad ideas incorporated in other parts of the engine. For instance, I thought the plugs to allow inspection of the valve heads *in situ* in the steam chest was a good idea, but when I saw a fitter taking yards of cotton waste out of the oil trays of the leading wheels, I did not hand the U.S.A. railroads a medal for that archaic method of keeping a journal lubricated.

If I had little experience of the American engines I'm sorry I cannot say the same about the G.N. "D1" class. Like many of the engines which came north to "assist" the L.N.E.R. Scottish Area, they were not in new condition; far from it, in fact, and to our other problems was added the feat of trying to maintain and operate "foreign" engines which were nearly obsolete when we got them.

If I ever want to claim credit for heroic conduct I think I'll plump for the moments I spent with the "Ponies," as the "D1s" were nicknamed. Nowadays I suppose I would say they carried a "gremlin," for I'm sure they were inhabited by a spirit of devilry which delighted in keeping both driver and fireman on their toes.

Their decrepit injectors required constant attention, and the throttle and reverser were a source of nuisance from start to finish of the trip, the former because it was designed to shut the moment you took both hands from it (a thumb screw to hold it in position was generally missing), while the screw which kept the reversing lever notched up had a habit of slacking back. When that happened with the "Pony" galloping along at seventy miles an hour, the handle of the reverser could quite easily break an arm or a leg as it rotated into full fore gear, with a speed and force which nothing could resist.

Life was never dull on a "Pony." It had a diabolical repertoire of kicks, twists, and bucks, that put the mustangs of the cowboys rodeos into the amateur class. When piloting an East Coast express it was just a case of hanging on, and hoping the reversing lever wouldn't suddenly bash your ribs in. In my time I was tattooed black and blue all over from the playful antics of the G.N. "D1."

To see my fireman lifting water at speed was an entertainment in itself. The water scoop handle was a long lever which he pulled out from the tender end to drop the scoop into the water trough. Once the water gripped that scoop, no human power could get it out again until the end of the trough was reached. This did not prevent the strong ones trying; that is, they tried it once, and that was enough. The "Pony" entered into the fun of the game, and the strong one suddenly found no resistance to his efforts. Both the lever and himself would shoot forward, while from the tender filler hole a cascade of water would descend on the coal and an avalanche would pour into the cab almost knee-deep.

After that experience it was more comfortable to wait until you were two-thirds of the way across the troughs, "dip" the scoop and flick the lever shut at the end. Half a tank of water was ample to take a "D1" to Newcastle on her own. If she was piloting another engine, of course, this let you out and so far as I was concerned I frequently ran the 125 miles between Edinburgh-Newcastle piloting an express on one tank of water with a "Pony."

To put it mildly, the super-secrecy of the wartime security measures (as interpreted by my shedmaster at Haymarket) was good. Now and again I'd be told: "You are taking a train from so-and-so shortly; look in for instructions tomorrow." When "tomorrow" came I would call at his office and be informed that I better have a look to refresh my memory of a divergence from a regular route.

So off I would go and have a look at a few miles of railway over which I possibly hadn't worked a train for a year or so. I'd go back to the "gaffer" and report. Then I would be told to turn out at a certain time, and possibly when I would be almost leaving the shed, he would blandly inform me that the train was running on a different route to the one I thought. If Hitler's "Fifth Column" ever got any information in Scotland, it certainly wasn't from Haymarket shed. He was good, was that "gaffer," and I appreciated his caution.

I don't know whether it was this kind of "hush-hush" that was responsible or not, but it is true that on one occasion it very nearly landed General Eisenhower's train in a coal siding. I don't know what went wrong with the arrangements for "belling" this train on from one signalbox to another, but whatever it was, as we approached a little wayside box with only a station and a coal siding to justify its existence, the distant signal was "on" and the points and the signal for the siding were all set for our reception.

For once I refused to obey the rule book instruction which says that a driver must obey all signals whether he knows the reason for the signal indication or not. I kept the whistle going and the train crawling along to give that signalman a chance to realise that "someone had blundered" and that this was not the local goods which "lifted and left" traffic once daily.

That lad in the box "cottoned on" all right, for I could hear the slam of the ground signal and the points being reversed a good hundred yards away. The "home" and "advance" signals were jerked off more quickly than I've ever seen, and I grinned to reassure a worried-looking face which watched our passing. The throttle was wide open again and I was going to recover the lost time. No harm was done, the train shortly after reached its destination on time, and as I watched Ike's tall form dominating the reception party gathered to meet him, I wondered what he would have thought if at that moment he had been looking out on a sylvan scene from a wayside coal siding.

It's well known now, of course, that Scotland saw many important war leaders traversing its length by railway train, and I've watched "Monty" deep in conversation with high-ranking military officers not a dozen yards from the cab of my engine. Field-Marshal Montgomery had *this* in common with most great men, he never seemed to be too harassed to remember the ordinary fellows around him. I've seen him obviously deep in thought and discussion with another officer walking past my engine, but as he passed the cab his hand would rise in a gesture that showed he was aware of my presence even if he never looked in my direction.

At times like those I felt, as I've often felt, that the cab of a locomotive was an ideal place from which to observe humanity. The engine seems to give a sense of anonymity to the driver, and he, like Kipling, could say that what he sees proves that "the Colonel's Lady an' Judy O'Grady are sisters under their skin." That could stand for the General and the private as well.

It was certainly a privilege to stand at a railway platform at the head of a train and know that in the train was the commander of the British Army sitting perhaps in conference, with the telephones on the table linking him to any part of the world. It gave me a boost, too, that when I got home and my wife asked casually what had kept me late, I just as casually answered "technical hitches again." This was our formula for indicating: "Ask no questions and you'll be told no lies." It was good to think that one was trusted.

Quite a few of these trips, however, were made in the blackout, when all one saw was a few ghostly figures quietly leaving the train, and disappearing into the enveloping darkness. Who they were I never queried, nor even wanted to know. In fact the less I did know during the war the more comfortable I felt, and curiously enough I was comfortable at least in mind, in the wartime black-out.

The blackout, while a nuisance in many ways, was a real boon while actually running a train. It took a war to let me fully understand how very many difficulties a driver encountered in running during the hours of darkness. For instance, on a particular high-speed stretch on the up Aberdeen road as we rounded a curve at something like 70mph, away on the straight ahead were no fewer than twenty-one green lights. One of those green lights might be my "distant" signal. The remainder of them were a clutter of fancy lamps illuminating a new housing scheme.

Just before the war each new housing area seemed to compete with the other in experimental lighting, and the spot I have mentioned had chosen lights which blended and formed a perfect match for the signal I was so anxious to see. The point here was the fact that my signal light might be out, and it was only when quite near that I could satisfy myself it was in order. The black-out cured this sort of thing during the war, but it is now worse than ever, with the rash of neon signs and super illumination that has broken out in all parts of Britain, apparently regardless of the difficulties experienced by my fraternity on high-speed engines.

As an aid to the wartime black-out our engines had to conform to regulations, and my first attempt to obliterate the searchlight beam from the firebox nearly suffocated me. My engine cab was shrouded in tarpaulin which draped itself in unlovely folds from the cab to the tender. The glass side windows were removed and replaced by iron sheets. More tarpaulin was hitched to both cab doors, and I was told: "Military observers are going to watch you on the Forth Bridge. If there's as much as a peep of light escaping, you'll be possibly shot at dawn, or at least there will be a heck of a row". So I made sure there wasn't a chink in the black-out armour on that engine.

Unfortunately, to trap the light meant also trapping the heat, and for more than ten minutes my fireman and I lived in the equivalent of a baker's oven. I never knew that my spare, not to say skinny, form carried so much water content until I felt it rolling down my spine and coming almost out at my boots.

Although we were on the bridge proper for only three minutes, I tied those tarpaulin sheets securely in place a good five minutes before reaching the point where the military lads would be taking note, and suffered it out for a few miles after passing over. That was all we could stand, before letting in a rush of air via the cab doors. When I went home that night and got into a bath my skin from neck to toes was covered with a red rash that wouldn't have disgraced the ripest strawberry, and for days I regretted it wasn't now the custom to scratch oneself in public.

Those war days were full of experiment and efforts to solve hitherto unheard-of problems. We got instructions on how to immobilise the engines in case "Jerry" suddenly appeared on our footplates, and that set off some real heroics amongst members of the older school. This included everything from detonators to scalding oil and water, if any invader dared to step upon their sacred engines.

It was all a bit confusing, if not exactly funny, considering that most of us prior to the war hadn't a great deal of good to say regarding the common user engine. The war appeared to alter this attitude completely. Any engine, in fact any bit of railway, became an almost proprietorial thing to most of us.

So we joined the local volunteers and eventually blossomed out into Home Guard uniforms which made us look like real soldiers. We prowled around sheds and other railway property in case any saboteurs took it into their heads to show up. I'm sure a few of the more blood-thirsty secretly hoped to try out their marksmanship. Those of us who knew one end of a rifle from the other found ourselves in sudden demand and the possessors of military rank in our off moments.

Bill MacLeod and I, who had been both army instructors during World War 1, were offered instructors' jobs with the army at Derby. We turned the offer down flat. Both of us felt we would be more useful where we were. Bill eventually became a captain in charge of a Home Guard armoured train which patrolled part of the East Coast, while I resurrected all the old "gen" about morse, semaphore, and "what have you" on signalling and communication and even put some of my colleagues through physical jerks, much to their ribald amusement. "Big Steve" stuck his medal ribbons up once more and became a hard-boiled Sergeant-Major in his off time, while Jock Todd spent most of his off duty working on the engine which hauled the armoured train around. It was all a bit fantastic. We ran trains (bombs or no bombs), we did without sleep to do our Home Guard stint, and in between found time to do some "back-room boy stuff."

So far as I was concerned the war years and a few years after sorted themselves into something of a pattern, where I spent my time driving express trains for a period, then doing a job which normally fell to the technical or inspectorial grades. Then back I went to the footplate for a spell and so on.

The fact was that I was being found out. Those years I had spent putting something "under my hat" weren't known to many. One of those who did know, however, was Jock Bartholomew, who was by this time Chief Locomotive Inspector for the Scottish Area of the L.N.E.R., and I rather fancy that he had a good deal to do with my wartime activities.

XVII

The "Why" is Important

I've always considered that the actual driving of a locomotive is merely the end to the interest an engineman finds in his job. In the many screeds I've written about engine driving I have now and again indulged in a little metaphorical nonsense. More than once I have indicated that *Spearmint* and myself held heart-to-heart conversations. But I took it for granted that the reader would very rightly put these alleged communings prosaically into proper perspective. What was actually happening between my engine and myself was my urge to diagnose a symptom disclosed to me in much the same way as a patient does to a doctor, telling him what he feels from some hidden irritation to his physical well-being.

To me this forms a very large part of the many years of enjoyment I have had from my job, and to enjoy it to the full it is very necessary that an engineman should recognise the importance of the "why." He's got to be "nosey" about the function of everything on, in, and about, his engine, and right now I'd like to give a practical instance or two of what I mean.

During the war the Gresley "V2s" at Haymarket were giving trouble with their sands. It was all rather mysterious. The drivers kept booking the gravity sands "not working," but when the fitters examined them there was no blockage, the valves were in perfect working order, the pipes were clear, the rods and connections to the handle in the cab were in order. When the sands were tried out in the shed they worked perfectly, but whenever the engines started to climb the banks on the Aberdeen or Carlisle roads those sanders just did not put sand on the rails.

I drove several "V2s" on these roads and the gradients are such that sands are really a *must,* especially on sections overhung by trees or in deep cuttings during the autumn and winter, where fallen leaves and frost make for bad rail conditions. Whenever a "V2" got her nose elevated on such up gradients the sands stopped running.

As usual there was hefty "knitting of the brows" over this, to say nothing of a few "cracks" with my shedmaster. We came to the conclusion that the shape of the sand pipes on the "V2" was the cause of the trouble. We thought that because of the cramped space the bends in the pipes were so angled that when the engine was standing on the level the sand would run down the pipes but whenever the engine tilted her nose upwards the angle of the bends in the pipes became such that they attained the "angle of repose" at which sand came to rest.

This was pure conjecture, and without some proof nobody would be keen on curing the trouble. So, aided and abetted by the shedmaster, I decided to try out a quiet experiment on my own, and before very long had elapsed the Mutual Improvement classroom housed a secret apparatus.

I rigged up on a board a series of glass tubes attached to a miniature sand box. The tubes were bent and angled to the same degrees as those on the "V2." A dial with a pointer was connected, with degrees calibrated to approximate to that of the tilt an engine would assume in climbing various gradients.

It worked beautifully. As the sand ran through those glass tubes, while the apparatus was kept on the level, it could be seen how it slowed up at the bends in the pipes, but it still kept running. Whenever the slightest tilt was given, as if the engine was on a bank, the sand simply refused to pass the pipe bend, even although the angle was still a few degrees in a downward direction. In other words we could *see* that sand, unlike water, did not continue running until it reached its own level.

Both the shedmaster and myself became fascinated with this experiment. We fixed up a full sized sand box complete with valves and pipe, and carried out a whole series of tests with sand heated to different temperatures, and most of this fun and games went on in our own time. I had quite often to ask that shedmaster if he hadn't a home to go to, when we suddenly found it was nine or ten o'clock at night, and we should have been at home some three hours earlier.

I don't know what the result of that experiment was, or whether it was reported further afield or not, but what we found out in the Mutual Improvement classroom was put to good use at Haymarket, and I believe cured, to a large degree, the trouble hitherto experienced with the sands of the "V2s." Where before the pipes were nearly flattened with constant hammering in an effort to induce the sand to flow, they now remained rounded, but the contortions which they had to make to bring them from the sand box to the rail were now altered to give them the maximum degree of "fall" that space permitted.

When I got *Spearmint* as my regular engine, among the first jobs to which I attended was the exhaust injector. For the benefit of the uninitiated let me explain. The so-called "exhaust" injector should really be described as the "live and exhaust steam automatic injector," for it injects water into the boiler with both forms of steam. In other words, when the engine is standing or running with the throttle shut, steam coming direct from the boiler is used, but whenever the throttle valve is opened and a certain pressure is in the exhaust steam, the injector uses a proportion of this steam to do the job.

The pipe which carries the exhaust steam to the injector apparatus under the cab runs from the smokebox and has a "shut-off" cock, which I've always considered an inducement to lazy maintenance. It was too easy to shut off and make the injector a fully "live" steam one. I believe by doing this some eight to twelve per cent. more coal and water is used, but the "couldn't care less" chap isn't normally bothering about that. When an exhaust pipe union was blowing or the pipe was fractured, turning that "shut-off" cock was an easier solution to the problem than effecting a cure.

So I saw to it that *Spearmint* wasn't robbed of the benefits of a perfectly working exhaust injector, and I was able to do that largely because of my experience with that fairly complicated apparatus during the war. Maybe it was because of the many bits and pieces it contained, or maybe because of natural cussedness on my part to understand the function or "bust." Whatever it was, I almost "lived" inside the Class H. injector until it started to "speak" back to me. I "borrowed" all the "internals" from the store at odd times, and amused myself and my mates in the M.I.C. by building up the bits on the table and then faking defects. From these "fakes" I used to try and diagnose just what symptoms would be given by the injector on the road, and the "classroom defects," weren't these mentioned in the book of words on the subject of exhaust injectors.

For months I spent an hour or two in the classroom after finishing my shift, very often in the company of interested wartime fitters, who had not served their time as locomotive mechanics, and were interested in the apparatus we used on railway engines. Gradually I found myself something of a specialist in diagnosing obscure complaints of the Class H. exhaust injector, and that obscure ailments could develop you can believe me.

For instance, there was the newly overhauled injector on a Gresley Pacific which just would not work. Four times it was dismantled and not a thing could be spotted which pointed the way to a cure. Four different fitters at as many different depots had tried it, and they were all satisfied that there was nothing functionally wrong with the apparatus. Every part was apparently in order, while the steam, water, and boiler "paths" were found on test to be all right.

Of course, I was more than interested in the mystery, and one of the fitters knew it. "Here is something you won't cure, 'Mac'," was all he said, and of course he knew how I reacted to any challenge like that. "Let's tear it apart, and what's the betting I don't spot what's wrong." I said. This was sheer bravado on my part. I hadn't a clue to the solution, in fact I'd never driven the engine since the injector had been overhauled.

Joe was all for it, and was soon going through the drill adopted by a fitter who is intent on examining the Class H. injector. He drew out the combining cone, split new and shining brass. He examined it, looked at the two cones it contained, tested the hinged flap; he even put the flap through a rough and ready "light test" to see that the face of it fitted that on the body of the cone.

"Nothing wrong with that lot," he commented, handing it to me, and I was about to agree with him, when I noticed something. The gap between the two cones seemed smaller—ever so little smaller than the gap I had been used to seeing in my M.I.C. discussions. I knew just why that gap must be a particular size, no more, or no less. It was there to create a degree of vacuum without which the injector wouldn't work.

That was all that was wrong. Apparently the small renewable tip which controlled the size of the gap had become jammed (possibly because of a bad thread) and in the assembling this had misled the fitter who did the job into thinking this was screwed tight home. Nobody had thought of the function, although it was all there in the book of words for those who were interested. I've already said it's the "why" which makes this job of mine so interesting, so before deserting the subject I'd like briefly to sketch the way an engine "speaks" to a driver as she runs the road, and how he replies to her "conversation."

Assuming I were to take charge of an entirely strange engine and set off on an express trip, from the moment I open the throttle I start to learn about her "character." For it is true that being in the company of a strange engine assumes all the facets of hob-nobbing with a newly made human acquaintance.

From the first few exhaust beats at the chimney I sense whether her "character" is bright or sluggish, and as the driving wheels continue to revolve at increasing speed, I feel under my feet the action of the springs, as the cab floor responds to the effect from the thrust of the pistons and the antagonism to that thrust from the load on the tender draw-bar.

I like to feel an even rhythm to those first heavy efforts. If I don't, I mentally assure my engine "I'll have a look at your springs when we get to the end of the trip." And I not only look, but give the plates of the laminated springs a tap with a hammer and watch for movement at the centre "buckle," where a plate can be broken and remain hidden. As I'm looking at the springs I also look at the "rubbing marks" made by the driving boxes as they slide in the guides. This tells me an awful lot about the action of the springs.

When we pass a lift of wagons in an adjoining siding, they form an ideal sounding board for engine and engineman communing. The big and little ends on that side assume a different tone of voice from the others, and I don't even need to look to know that there's a knock on this particular big end. Again I take suitable action at journey's end.

As the speed increases and we belt over a junction crossing, I'm watching the chimney top (not, as my fireman seems to think, for black smoke). I'm watching the chimney to see its behaviour as we "cross the crossings." If it bobs up and down to the contour of the rails with a "rounded effect" I'm satisfied the engine is properly balanced on the springs, but if it "dips" into the hollows then I'm having a look at her when I get her on a turntable, and I am looking to see if she is "down on the nose." I have seen a bad running engine cured like magic by the simple turning of a few nuts which made each of the springs carry their proper weight.

I would like to expand a little on this theme for the benefit of the many "amateur enginemen" who have written me and suggested that they have the same feeling when driving their cars as I have when operating a Pacific engine. Before doing so let me say that I know something about the internal combustion engine.

There is really no similarity between the "feel" a driver experiences with a railway engine and that which a motor vehicle driver obtains. In spite of the fact that a Pacific engine weighs over 160 tons as compared with the few hundredweights of a car, there is a greater degree of intimacy experienced by the engineman. When I start watching the chimney top crossing a junction I am doing so to verify a bad running engine. There's an awful lot of things which can make an engine run badly, as there are a *lot of ways* in which an engine can be *said* to run badly. This is where the diagnosis depends on the sensitivity of that "feel" which exists on the footplate as on no other form of power unit. The following will possibly illustrate this point better than a book full of scientific talk.

In a previous chapter I have said that whenever possible I took a look at the train brake to make sure *all* the brake blocks were clear of the wheels. This wasn't always possible when connections from Aberdeen or Glasgow were tied on to the rear of the night expresses to London just before starting time.

On one of these trains I wasn't happy about the way we were getting along the road. There was nothing much to it (so little, in fact, that my fireman did not know any difference in the working of the engine). On the stretches where we should have been sailing along like a bird, I felt that lack of "gay abandon", which could have been imagination on my part.

At Berwick, our first stop, we were booked to take three minutes, I saw to it that we had another three on top of that and during the six minutes which we stood at the station I had doubled up the train and back to the cab (it wasn't such a long train, fortunately), after fully releasing a brake on one of the rear coaches. One of the blocks was no more than merely touching the wheel tyre.

It wasn't bad distribution of the weight on the springs that time, I knew, because the engine was wasting no effort in "sideways motion." She kept going straight ahead, yet she told me that something was keeping her from performing better than she was, and I cannot think of any better way of describing how she told me, except that expression I so often use—it was just the "feel" of the engine.

In trying to explain this communing between a steam locomotive and her driver, I'm not referring to the obvious symptoms which are plain to everyone, such as, say, an engine "off the beat" where the exhaust proclaims to high heaven that the steam distribution to the pistons is "haywire." What I'm trying to get across is the sympathetic understanding which could turn "just another engine" into something a little better than the rest of her kind, if one could only see the results of what is booked in the repair card.

That's where the driver of a regular engine scores. He can follow up his ideas, and see if the repairs he books cures the diseases he has diagnosed. Having said that I feel I had better get off the subject.

The common user engine and all it means is a long-standing sore point with me, so let's return to the "back-room boy" stuff.

During the war one of the biggest problems faced by the railways was that of maintenance, and anything that could help to keep the wheels turning was welcome. Oil was a big factor in this respect, and oil wasn't easy to come by when sea transport was so vital for our survival.

That is why the rape oil content disappeared from the lubricating oil specification for railway engines. Rape seed came from India, and the precious rape oil that we so lavishly used in the pre-war days was now required to make margarine. I believe the best oil for locomotive bearings prior to the war was a blend of 75 per cent. mineral and 25 per cent. rape oil.

So when my District Superintendent told me to carry out an exhaustive practical test of a new oil, and showed me the description of that oil I knew what had happened. The description read "½ per cent. Olein Content," and I grinned as my mind went back over fifteen years. Perhaps it was the grin which made him ask: "Know anything about that? "Yes," was all I said, and we got down to the details of the test. I was still grinning when I left that office, for I had already made up my mind that here was an opportunity I'd been waiting for.

I was all set to go to town on this test. What my Superintendent didn't know at the time (and it's questionable if he even knows it now), was that he'd handed me something on a plate which I would have been willing to do in my spare time, free gratis, and for nothing. As it was, he agreed to pay me inspectorial rates, and after the test was completed handed me an honorarium as a "token of appreciation from the L.N.E.R. for services rendered." (The accountant, however, cannily deducted the income tax from the money before I received it).

But to return to that "½ per cent. Olein Content" and the reason for the grin. Some fifteen years before, I had been nosing into the "whys" of lubrication, and as usual I wasn't content to accept a bald statement in the text book. I wanted to know the reason why "rape oil had a high viscosity." So when I read "½ per cent. Olein Content" I recognised at once my old friend of fifteen years' standing, "Oleic Acid," the free acid in rape oil which gives it its terrific power of clinging to a bearing without sheeting under the knife edge thrust of tons when a heavy engine "takes the load."

When I first read about it, the extraction of the free acid from the oil was not considered a commercial possibility, but war had apparently changed all that, and both the margarine manufacturers and the lubrication oil blenders were now reaping the benefits from scientific progress. That is what I deduced when I answered "yes" to the question my Superintendent asked me, and that is why I "went to town" on this test. I assumed that the "½ per cent. Olein Content" was taking place of that bulk 25 per cent. rape oil, and I was curious to see how it worked out in practice.

At Haymarket I was given a Gresley Pacific to act as the "guinea pig" and for two days, with drivers and fitters, I got her prepared. Yes, it took all of two days completely to drain every drop of oil from every oil box, tray, and mechanical pump, and to renew the worsted trimmings and steel pins in the big ends. When that was completed to my satisfaction (and I was hard to satisfy) I carefully measured one hundred pints of that "½ per cent. Olein Content" oil into the various places which were now bone dry, and I told the "gaffer" the engine was set to commence the test.

By the end of three months, I had followed that engine into almost every part of the L.N.E.R. system where a Gresley Pacific penetrated from Haymarket. She was given to a variety of drivers on the East Coast expresses, and she went to Carlisle, Glasgow, Perth, and Dundee. Wherever she went I was sitting in the train behind her. At the "in-between," as well as the terminal stops, I took measurements and temperatures. This was what I was asked to do, but as usual I wanted to do a little more for my own inquisitive satisfaction.

As I experimented with different sizes of pins in the big ends, and with various types of worsted trimmings in the oil boxes, I knew that what I reported would be subjected to laboratory tests by the L.N.E.R. chemists at Stratford.

So privily, and in utter secrecy, I rigged up another apparatus which not only gave me fair viscosity tests, but cut down the normal "syphoning time test" taken by a trimming in an oil box from some eighteen hours to the same number of minutes. Fifteen years before I had wanted to do all this, I did manage to carry out quite a few "laboratory" tests but I never dreamed that I would have all the resources of the L.N.E.R. placed at my disposal to line up a real practical test—the ideal way, in my opinion, of proving anything.

Each night I verified on my home-made "laboratory" the practical results I was getting on the engine, and these results were proving the new blending of oil first rate. Before finishing the test, the Pacific big ends (each of which hold exactly one pint) were running 500 miles on one filling, and the pins fitted were such that there was still a quarter of a pint of oil left at the end of the 500 miles. That gives a fair idea of how good was this oil.

It was nearing the end of the oil trial and I was busy carrying out a few final tests in the Mutual Improvement classroom where I had my home-made apparatus, when into the room walked my chief, his assistant, and the chemist from Stratford. That tore it. I tried to stand in front of the thing I had rigged up and you could have seen my blushes a mile away. Here was a real live chemist used to all the sophistications of a well-fitted laboratory, and here was I trying to tell him something which I was getting from an amateurish apparatus which in actual cash had cost me 4s. 6d.

Mr. Hill the chemist, however, was kindness itself. He insisted on me explaining how I got my results, thanked me for my reports, and left with the others. "That," I thankfully said "is that." I was just starting to breathe freely again when I was called to the 'phone.

"Bring that apparatus of yours to the District Superintendent's office," a voice said, and when I got there I was told I had to carry on for another fortnight taking a further series of tests and in collaboration with the Assistant District Superintendent make graphs of the results. These were included in my final reports. This final phase was carried out in the Assistant District Superintendent's office.

I'm still wondering if any other driver has ever walked about for a fortnight with the key of the office of his Assistant District Superintendent in his pocket, for that's what I did during those fourteen days. Those days not only proved interesting in themselves but provided me with adequate proof that it was changed days indeed from those of my early experience of railway officialdom. I think the name for it is democracy.

XVIII
GOODBYE TO "SPEARMINT"

Just before the Battle of Britain I became a Controller for a brief period. The war traffic between England and Scotland had developed different channels of "flow" and engines had a habit of disappearing from their depots once they set off on a train. There was no knowing where they would finish up, and it was necessary to set up some kind of organisation which could keep track of them, and if possible assist to a greater use of engine power without useless light running when an attempt was made to return the engines to their home depots.

So three drivers, of whom I was one, were given the job of working out some form of Engine Control. We were given the rough idea and told to work it out in conjunction with Controllers in adjoining areas. We were, of course, a foreign element injected into the control room, which was manned by clerical grades, and our practical answers to the problems which arose maybe amused them. Quite often, I'm sure, we shocked their more refined administrative minds, but gradually they became used to us, and in fact told us they were sorry to see us go once we got the Control running and handed over.

I certainly enjoyed the experience, if it was for nothing more than to be able to pay a tribute to a much maligned band of railwaymen. The Controllers, as almost any unthinking locomotiveman will tell you, "just don't know what they are talking about." Those same unthinking ones should have had my experience and then they would maybe change their tune.

As I am writing this, in my mind's eye I can see one of my temporary colleagues, big one-armed Andrew Black (he lost his arm in World War I in action with the Cameron Highlanders). I can see Andrew, his right shoulder hunched to hold the telephone to his ear, directing, directing, directing: finding paths for trains, dealing with a block caused by a derailment, while four or five signalmen were all wanting to know at once what they were going to do with this "blankety-blank" goods when every siding was jammed with trains and traffic.

Andrew, with the full picture of all the trains in his area, to say nothing of German bombers flying here and there, would find the answers like a master chess player. Not once but many nights he never left his desk, not even for a cup of tea. With the control room like an oven, with the steel shutters clamped tight over the windows, I would have given a lot to be outside on the footplate in the fresh air, but Andrew didn't seem to notice.

Now and again he would shout down to me: "Here's one of your pals, Mac" and I'd depress the appropriate key which brought the 'phone call on to my little exchange, to hear an irate voice telling the world "I've been on duty four hours, how about relief for food? You so-and-so Controllers don't care a damn—"

I would look down the room at Andrew, intent now on more serious business, and instead of saying "Oh, go to hell!" I would argue with sweet reasonableness with Sandy or Jock or Tom. Because they knew me as one of themselves they would believe me, but "these blasted controllers, no!" How I longed to kick a few of my mates in the pants during that brief period I spent at the receiving end of a control telephone. Just a few of them though, the unthinking ones: very often I was proud of them.

For instance, there was that night the order came that when the "red" was flashed to all signalboxes, the German raiders were too near, and all trains must stop. The "red" was on, everything was bogged down, when almost together the 'phones went, and from all over our area, drivers were telling the controllers "Germans or no Germans we're going to get these trains moving. Tell your signalmen to pull off the 'boards'." From then on there was no attention paid to that "stop" war signal, and the trains kept moving.

My control job completed, I returned thankfully to the footplate, but I had learned about something to which I had not previously given much thought.

Andrew Black died a young man. I think as I watched him in that control room I witnessed the reason for his untimely death.

In between driving express trains I would occasionally come off the footplate and spend a few days speaking words of wisdom to the youngsters who were joining the service. Now and again I would take a few lads from the cleaning squad and put them through their paces prior to their registration as firemen. In those days we had no firing instructors on the L.N.E.R. in Scotland so far as I am aware, so I may be able to claim that I was the forerunner of this type before they were officially appointed. Until they were appointed I enjoyed every minute in the Mutual Improvement classroom with those lads.

I'm afraid my methods weren't strictly in accordance with the orthodox official ideas, quite apart from the fact that I'm still unaware whether what I was doing was strictly an official job, or whether it was a local move by my go-ahead shedmaster to give training and some sort of locomotive sense to his embryo firemen. Mixed with the rules and regulations, the simple mechanics of the locomotive, and the firing instruction generally, I drew from my own background of experience, where I found other things of assistance to me in making life easier on the footplate. I expounded on the benefits of physical training, and this led inevitably to more than talking in the M.I.C. I had those lads running on the track, swimming, and boxing.

At the end of their short period of training I set them a written examination, and passed them on to the shedmaster for his final approval, but that wasn't the end of our contact. Off duty, we foregathered, an increasing band of enthusiasts, and in between our sing-songs, our dances, and our athletics we talked engines, and not one of those youngsters let me down. Each of them passed the examination with flying colours.

The regular meetings of the M.I.C. became more alive than ever, and I now see the boys I trained making good as the coming enginemen of tomorrow. I'll always look back on this "back-room" chore as not only rewarding but very revealing. For it gave me an insight into the character of the rather inarticulate product which is called "modern youth."

They weren't angels, and I didn't want them that way, but some of their goings on stretched my powers of advocacy pretty near to breaking point. I knew, of course, that it was more or less their kind of humour.

For instance, there was that matter of the four pianos which disappeared from a city salvage dump. The police were sure that it was the work of our boys, as the dump lay across the main line from Haymarket. I had a word with the lads. They looked shocked at the very idea; butter couldn't have melted in their mouths. So I went, all indignant, and told the shedmaster what I thought about the suspicions of the police. Then the pianos were found a fortnight later neatly parked inside the bomb shelters at either end of the shed.

How the young devils had managed to manhandle those unwieldy musical instruments up a steep bank and across four sets of main line rails and through a shed simply swarming with men without being spotted, I'll never know. Neither would anybody have discovered the pianos had their love of music not given them away.

I could even find it in me to regret that they were found out, for there can be little wrong with lads who find enjoyment in hammering out Beethoven, even if it's done on an instrument with half the keys missing. For this I could say with truth, that they were better men than I was at the same age. I found out long ago, however, that music and engine driving have a lot in common. Maybe that's why my shedmaster facetiously dubbed me "The Child Welfare Officer."

In 1949 I went to the Isle of Man to spend my holidays watching the speed aces hurtling round the roads in the Tourist Trophy motor cycle races. From Arthur Bourne, one-time Editor of *The Motor Cycle,* I got a good deal of assistance in this. Not only had I the opportunity of having a "crack" with most of the top-notchers in this hectic game, but I was given the freedom of the Press stand and other facilities to enable me to compile an article on the subject. That last sentence is the clue to why I said goodbye to *Spearmint.*

In my young days I had two over-riding ambitions. I wanted to write—the writing "bug" was, I think, ingrained in the very marrow of my bones—I also wanted to drive express engines. Obviously it was sheer presumption (at least I thought so at the time) for a youngster to aspire to write anything which anybody else would want to read, so the writing phobia was shoved into the 'secret vice' category. It became a hobby, an outlet and medium of expression which no one but myself read, quite apart from the fact that if I wanted to drive engines, I must be prepared to make that my life's work.

As I've already indicated, I was not a natural engineman like "Swannie" or many of my colleagues. I had no railway background to urge me to carry on a tradition. My father was a fisherman from the Island of Harris. He never even saw a railway until he came to the mainland of Scotland. He couldn't even speak English when he first landed. Gaelic was his ordinary everyday language, as it was my mother's, who, however, was bi-lingual. I just can't explain why I had such an urge for the footplate, unless it was that which I suppose every youngster had, a sense of hero-worship.

I certainly had that to a high degree after reading something about George Stephenson and his indomitable fight against odds— that uneducated lad, who, at eighteen years of age, could neither read nor write, but who lived to say; "I am now called George Stephenson Esq., of Tapton House, near Chesterfield ... . I have dined with princes, peers, and commoners, with persons of all classes, from the humblest to the highest. I have dined off a red herring when seated in a hedge-bottom, and I have gone through the meanest drudgery. I have seen mankind in all its phases, and the conclusion I have arrived at is this,—that if we are all stripped, there is not much difference." He could say this after the members of a Royal Commission had described him "... this madman ... this Watt run wild," who wanted to build engines to run at ten to fifteen miles an hour. "A little better than an old horse trot," as George himself said, adding "I went on with my work regardless of them."

That was the sort of spirit which took my fancy as a boy—that and the fact that eventually the *Rocket* proved for all time that here was a revolution in transport, which in my young days had developed (so far as I was concerned) into the N.B. Atlantics.

My first time in London, the chief highlight of the occasion was a visit to the Science Museum, where I stood for long enough in front of the case containing among other Stephenson relics, his drawing instruments, which he kept wrapped in a piece of his wife's petticoat. That is how I felt about railway engines and the "father of all engine drivers." It is quite unexplainable, I admit, if heredity goes for anything, but my writing urge was easier to explain.

The generation to which my parents belonged came from that almost legendary period of over a hundred years ago, when the people of the Highlands of Scotland were natural story-tellers. They had little or no formal education, my mother being, I suppose, among the first who had reaped the benefits of normal schooling in bleak northern Caithness. Possibly my urge derived from this background of narrative with which I was familiar, and the fact that "high thinking and hard living" was considered an essential to the Highland mind in building up character. Be that as it may, I not only developed an inordinate appetite for reading, but had the dangerous urge to transmute the doings of my literary heroes into the realms of practical possibility. That perhaps accounts for my hero-worship of Robert Louis Stevenson, whose birthplace was within walking distance of my home.

By the time I reached the top link at Haymarket I was in a fair way to having a separate, and as I thought an undisclosed second career developing. For more than twenty years I had been writing under a pseudonym. By 1949, when I returned from the Isle of Man, I suppose I'd be right in saying that no other top link engineman was leading the Jekyll and Hyde existence I was doing.

I had just completed a 150,000 word history of the Associated Society of Locomotive Engineers and Firemen, I was writing regularly for American transport publications, while for nearly ten years I had been Scottish correspondent for the *Locomotive Journal*. For years I had been contributing to various papers in Scotland and across the border. Aided and abetted by Jim Swan, Jock Todd, and a bunch of enginemen from all over Britain, I was editing a semi-technical monthly magazine specially designed for locomotive-men, more or less as a hobby, to put our own ideas and experience as practical enginemen at the service of a wider circle of our colleagues.

By 1949, while I was driving top link express trains, I found that the writing "bug" had bitten me so deeply that I could no longer find the time to do the chores necessary to cope with my output. For some years I had had to have a "writing workshop" apart from my house with a typist to do my typing and cope with correspondents by then writing me from all over the world.

By 1949 it was about time I was making up my mind one way or the other, for it was obvious I was at the stage where I had to choose between *Spearmint's* throttle handle or an overworked pen. When I returned from the Isle of Man that June day, my mind was made up. I would stick to *Spearmint. I* just couldn't think of voluntarily chucking overboard all that engines and railways had given me for near forty years.

Fate must have been grinning all over. At least fate in the shape of Jock Todd was exercising his risible muscles in my office that day. For it was Jock who pointed the way to a solution of my problem.

Jock Todd and I had foregathered for our usual monthly crack on what should and should not be included in our monthly magazine, and there was an awful lot which we could *not* include. Locomotivemen are by-and-large averse to using a pen, but when they do let themselves go they are frank to the point of embarrassment. So we wielded a hefty blue pencil on occasions, such as when a fireman wrote about his "hashy" driver: "well here we go again, it's heads down and posteriors up ("posterior" wasn't the word he used).

We were busy on the job, when Jock suddenly said: "Seen the current vacancy list?"

"No," I said, "and you should know by this time I never look at that lure to the ambitious. *Spearmint* satisfies me and I'm looking for nothing higher."

"Well you should," said my instrument of fate, "there's a job advertised which seems made for you." And he slapped on my desk a copy of an item from the vacancy list, which is the railway equivalent of the "Situations Vacant" columns which the jobless or the ambitious scan in the Press. That was the first inkling I got that an Editor was required for the Scottish Regional edition of the *British Railways Magazine,* the job to which I was appointed in 1949.

So I said goodbye (or rather *au revoir)* to *Spearmint.* My horizon had widened. For years I'd been writing about locomotives and locomotivemen, not just my own engines and colleagues, but those from every part of Britain, for I had practised what I'd preached, and mingled with my fraternity to the widest extent. Only thus could I get a real line on the railways of Britain, and I use the word "railways" deliberately, for I had long ago realised that unless I tried to understand the job of other grades of railwaymen I could not get my views as an engineman into proper perspective.

I have said that the "why" is important, and have expanded on the locomotive angle, but there's a much wider "why" which embraces not only my railway colleagues, but the travelling public as well. Otherwise I would not need to explain to a layman friend of mine the "explosion" he called the sound of a set of Pacific "pop" safety valves blowing off suddenly with disastrous results to his daughter, convalescent after a serious illness. Those valves would have remained silent if the engineman concerned had thought beyond the narrow limits of his engine cab.

That is why I could say *au revoir* to *Spearmint* and shove my knees below the editorial desk. That is why I say my horizon had widened, in a fashion which allowed me to "eat my cake and have it as well."

When nostalgia gets the better of me, I pull a suit of dungarees out of a cupboard, take a ride on the footplate, and write an article for the *B.R. Magazine.* Only occasionally does that happen, however, for now I've got every phase of railways to write about and enjoy; and you can tell the world the operative word in that last sentence is "enjoy."

Conclusion

In every book I have written (this is the fourth), I have said that when I have finished the last chapter I had a sense of not saying all I wanted to say. It is a common feeling, I believe, with most writers. This book is no exception.

To the layman, the engine driver is a fellow who drives locomotives and nothing more. In point of fact he's possibly right in thinking that of a big number of them, but as I have tried to outline in this book, there's a lot more which concerns an engineman than driving engines. Several of these other facets of *life* on and off the footplate I have not touched upon here.

I have not discussed, for instance, the anomalies, the prejudices, or the criticisms which occasionally arise when a mishap or accident occurs. The views of the layman are very often different from those of the professional engineman. It has been my lot over a long number of years to make investigation into several major accidents in which my colleagues have been involved, and the "inside view" sheds a lot of light not seen by others.

I have said nothing (or next to nothing) about the so-called Modernisation of British Railways, as a practical railwayman looks at the proposals.

I have not mentioned the many foolishnesses of both management and men, which many years of experience as a staff representative have brought to my personal notice.

None of these things have found a place in this book, because they are fit items for an autobiography which can only be written at a certain time in one's life. While this book is largely biographical it is only so from one angle, and as I have said, an engineman's life is not solely concerned with driving locomotives.

Because this book is biographical it has flowed from under my hat with ease. I have enjoyed bringing out the highlights of memory, and, along with my colleagues, doing my best to verify the story which is told. Where verification has not been possible, I have written the final word, knowing from past experience that my readers will not apply the meticulous yard stick of the pedantic to a yarn which comes from a source which is never formal, and never intends to become so.

NORMAN McKILLOP
('Toram Beg')

Enginemen Elite

Perhaps the only British express driver who has exchanged the footplate for the editorial chair, Norman McKillop tells of a career which began on the North British in the rough, tough days in 1910 and culminated in his becoming one of the exclusive top link on the East Coast main line. He has been well described as at once a master and a lover of the locomotiveman's craft. To many he will be better known under the pseudonym of 'Toram Beg' that betokens his Gaelic parentage and explains the combination of the romantic and the practical in his nature evident in this narrative.

SHEPPERTON • MIDDLESEX

Handbook for Railway Steam Locomotive Enginemen

The burgeoning of the railway preservation movement all across the United Kingdom in the last 50 years has meant that there are now a considerable amount of steam locomotives preserved, maintained and in full working order and being run in frequent public service by preservation societies on heritage lines. This means that there is a continuing need for a practical handbook to help drivers and those responsible for maintaining the locomotives in safe condition for public use, covering all the basics of steam locomotive construction, technology and operation – this book fulfils that need admirably.

The book is a reprint of an official handbook issued for the education of and day-to-day use by British Railways enginemen in late 1957, when it was distributed to all members of the BR footplate grades concerned with steam power. In lucid terms, and with the aid of over 90 contemporary diagrams, many of which employ a variety of colours to distinguish, for example, saturated steam, superheated steam, exhaust steam, air, oil and water passages, the book provides an accessible guide to the basic principles of steam locomotive construction and operation.

ISBN: 9781800352889

Paperback, 200 pages **£20.00**

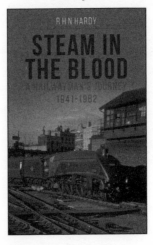

Steam in the Blood

A Railwayman's Journey 1941-1982

R.H.N. Hardy

Unlike many of his fellow managers, Dick was a rail enthusiast at heart and never lost his passion for locomotives and their crews. He considered himself first and foremost a 'people person' and estimated he had worked during his career with more than 25,000 men and women, many of whom became close friends and remained so for many years afterwards. After retirement in 1982, he made a major contribution to the continuance of main line steam train operations across the network.

This book is a welcome reissue of two of his autobiographical volumes outlining aspects of his illustrious railway career, Steam in the Blood and Railways in the Blood. These have been out of print for some years and their reissue in this competitively priced paperback edition, will bring the life and times of this remarkable railwayman to the attention of a new audience.

ISBN: 9781800351455

Paperback, 400 pages, **£9.95**

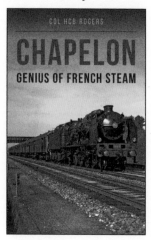

Chapelon

Genius of French Steam

Col HCB Rogers

The name Andre Chapelon will be known to everyone with an interest in the development of the steam locomotive. Put simply he was a genius, head and shoulders above all others in the field of steam locomotive design. This is not to belittle the skills and capabilities of men like Churchward, Stanier, Gresley and Bulleid. Indeed the latter acknowledged the influence of Chapelon on his work.

In his native France, Chapelon transformed the steam locomotives of various French railways from often mediocre machines into high performers surpassing the capabilities of similar machines used in other European countries at the time. He was responsible for both rebuilds as well as new designs. His work was disrupted by World War II, but his importance was reasserted in 1946 with his superb 4-8-4 No 242 A 1 capable of producing a continuous output of 5,500hp, a remarkable achievement.

Colonel Roger's book on Andre Chapelon, originally published in 1972, has been difficult to obtain for many years. It remains the best and most detailed biography of the man and his work. It is both a readable and accessible guide to the life and achievements of a man whom few would disagree was the foremost steam locomotive engineer the world has ever seen.

ISBN: 9781910809730

Paperback, 192 pages, **£8.99**

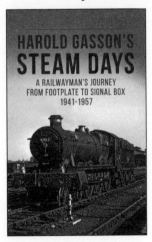

Harold Gasson's Steam Days

A Railwayman's Journey From Footplate to Signal Box 1941-1957

When Harold Gasson first put pen to paper more than forty years ago, it was at a time when there was a growing resurgence of interest in the steam railway.

Three of his books described his life as a fireman based at Didcot shed from the early 1940s. *Firing Days* was followed by *Footplate Days* and then *Nostalgia Days*. Finally, after Harold had forsaken the footplate for the signal box, came the final instalment, *Signalling Days*. All were eagerly sought after at the time for they described the railway readers wanted to hear about, providing a nostalgic perspective which could be enjoyed from the comfort of one's arm chair.

Out of print for several decades all four books have now been reprinted and are available together for the first time complete with a new set of illustrations. The steam engines and most of the mechanical signal boxes of Harold's working days may have been long consigned to history but in these well-written and enjoyable books they are brought vividly back to life for a new audience to enjoy as well for those who recall his era for whom these tales will reawaken treasured memories.

ISBN: 9781910809679

Paperback, 480 pages, **£9.99**